12/25/73

Mitchell —
    all my love,
        Theresa

the
**jazz**
scene

# the jazz scene

## Charles Fox

special photography by

## Valerie Wilmer

## Hamlyn

London  New York  Sydney  Toronto

*Front endpaper and title page Duke Ellington playing at the Newport Jazz Festival*

*Back endpaper John Lewis playing with the Modern Jazz Quartet*

*Jacket front Miles Davis*
*Jacket back Thelonious Monk*

Published by the Hamlyn Publishing Group Limited
London · New York · Sydney · Toronto
Hamlyn House, Feltham, Middlesex, England

© Copyright The Hamlyn Publishing Group Limited 1972

ISBN 0 600 02119 X

Filmset by Filmtype Services Limited, Scarborough, England
Text set in 9/10pt Monophoto Univers Light 685
Captions set in 9/10pt Monophoto Univers Light Italic 685

Reproduced and printed in Spain
by Printer, Industria Gráfica sa, Tuset 19
Barcelona, San Vincente dels Horts, 1972
Deposito Legal B 9551—1972
Mohn Gordon Ltd. London

# Contents

# New Orleans

Wandering round New Orleans in search of jazz history is a bit like reading *Ulysses* in Dublin. Street-names alone—Rampart, Perdido, Canal, Saratoga—can send a frisson down the spine. But just as not even the most dedicated James Joyce scholar will ever catch sight of Bloom lunching on burgundy and a gorgonzola sandwich in Davy Byrne's pub, so the kingdom of Buddy Bolden, Joe Oliver and Freddy Keppard has sidled into the past. A visitor armed with Tom Anderson's *Blue Book*, that guide to the raffishness of seventy years ago, can stroll along Basin Street, looking for Lulu White's Mahogany Hall or the Countess Willie Piazza's ('She has without doubt the most handsome and intelligent octoroons in the United States'), but find only garages and parking lots instead of the elegant parlours in which Jelly Roll Morton, Tony Jackson and the other ragtime professors once strutted their stuff. Even Congo Square, where the slaves used to dance on Saturday nights, has had its name changed to Beauregard Square, in honour of a brilliant but defeated Southern general. And those famous sons who are still alive mostly seem to live elsewhere: Zutty Singleton in New York, Albert Nicholas in Paris, Kid Ory in Hawaii.

Not that music is hard to run across in New Orleans. Electric guitars whine from doorways throughout the gaudy length of Bourbon Street. There are jazz clubs on Bourbon Street, too, including Al Hirt's and Pete Fountain's, but the neon tubes and the strippers outnumber the trumpeters and clarinettists, although old-time Dixie-landers like Sharkey Bonano and Johnny Wiggs's Bayou Stompers continue to make cheery sounds and Armand Hug goes on playing the piano year after year at the Golliwog Club, just off Canal Street. New Orleans has produced modern jazz players as well: some, like Ed Blackwell, Ornette Coleman's drummer, have upped and gone elsewhere; others, like the bandleaders Ellis Marsalis, Willie Tee and Fred Crane, stayed put. Even the avant-garde has an outpost in the French Quarter, not far from the river-front, at The Jazz Workshop and Listening Gallery on Decatur Street.

Hometowns have a habit of ignoring

*The Young Tuxedo Band takes to the streets for yet another New Orleans parade. Left Kid Ory, creator of the 'tailgate' trombone style, was leading his own band in New Orleans before World War I.*

their prophets, so it should come as no shock to discover that although three-quarters of the world thinks of New Orleans as the birthplace of jazz, the city's officials have—until fairly recently, that is—chosen to overlook the fact. ('We don't have anything on jazz,' a startled woman told the New Yorker's jazz critic, Whitney Balliett, when he called at the New Orleans Tourist Commission office in 1966.)

A big turn-about came in 1968, with the holding of the first week-long Jazzfest. And since the start of the 1960s there has been a local Jazz Museum, with Danny Barker—one-time guitarist in Cab Calloway's band, husband of blues-singer Blue Lu

Barker, a big-seller in the 1940s—helping to run it. Saunterers round the museum can stare at Bix Beiderbecke's cuff-links or the bugle that the thirteen-year-old Louis Armstrong blew at the Waifs' Home. But jazz pilgrims demand more than memorabilia. To cater for this New Orleans has what amounts to a pair of flesh-and-blood museums—Dixieland Hall and Preservation Hall.

Dixieland Hall occupies the Bourbon Street house that Lafcadio Hearn lived in before moving to Japan, while Preservation Hall, in nearby St Peter Street, is a typical French Quarter two-storey house, complete with elaborate wrought-iron balcony. Inside, both places are austere, serving no liquor, seating audiences on benches or in hard-back chairs, even—at Preservation Hall, anyway—making anyone who insists on hearing *The Saints* fork out a five-dollar tip. The musicians, all in their fifties or upwards, seem to turn up again and again in different permutations. Louis Cottrell, president of the local AFM branch and a deliciously rococo clarinettist, leads one of the bands; another is fronted by Jim Robinson, who used to play trombone with Bunk Johnson and George Lewis. Any of the groups could include Cie Frazier, perhaps the best old-style drummer left, or have Albert Burbank or Willie Humphrey on clarinet, while Sunday evenings often used to see Punch Miller putting in an appearance, still playing his trumpet in the cool, melancholy way he did just after the First World War when he arrived in New Orleans from the sugar-cane country. De De Pierce may blow some blues on his cornet while his wife, Billie, sings and plays piano, or 'Sweet Emma' Barrett—nicknamed 'The Bell Gal' because of the tiny bells sewn all over her dress and beret and garters—might be sitting at a piano, looking, to quote one bystander, 'as bony as a crow'. Emma, who was working with the Original Tuxedo Orchestra back in 1923, has been forced to sing more and play only as a duettist since a stroke paralyzed her right hand.

Hard-line purists have always looked on the saxophone as something of an upstart. In fact, saxophones were heard quite early on in New Orleans music (the turbulent Sam Morgan

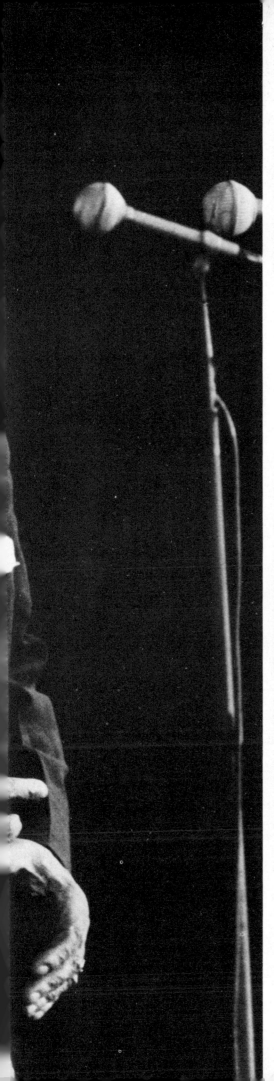

Left *Billie and De De Pierce, a husband-and-wife team who help to keep New Orleans blues alive.* Below

Two British jazzmen who made the pilgrimage to New Orleans: top *Keith Smith,* bottom *Ken Colyer.*

Band of the 1920s—with Jim Robinson on trombone, incidentally—used a pair of them). Yet, right up to his death in 1971, one of the liveliest musicians in the city—he trekked across Europe too—was Cap'n John Handy, an alto player whose style cross-referred to Benny Carter and Sidney Bechet and Earl Bostic but without sacrificing its autonomy. Another saxophonist is the tenor player Emanuel Paul, a long-time member of Kid Thomas's Stompers, the last of the regular bands to work the Negro dance halls, mostly in Algiers, on the other side of the Mississippi. Since the 1950s jobs have been hard to find—juke boxes, rock-and-roll, country-and-western, all have taken their toll—but Kid Thomas Valentine, seventy-five in 1971, still plays a fierce lead trumpet, the band still mixes pop standards—*Stardust, Summertime,* even waltzes and rumbas—with old war-horses like *Clarinet Marmalade* and the *Gettysburg March.*

When Kid Thomas's drummer, Sammy Penn, died in the winter of 1969, local Black Power supporters tried to stop him being given a traditional New Orleans funeral. For them the parade seemed just a piece of Uncle Tomming. But Penn had belonged to the Jolly Bunch, one of dozens of benevolent societies that flourish in New Orleans (others are the Elks, the Odd Fellows, the Six Ward Diamonds). They paid the funeral expenses, including the cost of a marching band. The night before burial, the body lay in the front room, surrounded by close relatives; the other mourners stayed in the back room, where they could smoke and drink. Next morning the procession threaded its way beneath fly-overs, the band occasionally drowned by motor horns or screeching brakes. Because it was a weekday and the musicians—nearly all part-timers—had jobs they must hurry back to, the band marched no more than three-quarters of a mile before 'turning the body loose'. On to the cemetery swept the hearse with attendant limousines; the band about-faced, broke into *Oh, Didn't He Ramble* and headed back to town.

Funerals of this sort are not peculiar to musicians; nor, despite Black Power pleas, is it only the elderly who parade. For just as a procession is headed by a marshal—it might be Danny Barker, wearing a bright floral sash, a white dove on his shoulder, a nine-inch cigar jutting from his mouth—the rear is always brought up by the 'Second Line', most of them young, strutting, dancing, cavorting, just as Louis and Jelly Roll did in their day. Many carry open umbrellas, gesturing, using them as ballet dancers might; the effect is very African, rather like a ritual rain-dance in Ethiopia. Even some of the younger Negro players march in the

bands (a Dizzy Gillespie phrase can get blurted out halfway through *Joe Avery's Blues*); a few Europeans take part too (the band at Sammy Penn's funeral included a Cockney clarinettist and a Swedish trombonist), for ever since Ken Colyer enlisted as a cook in the Merchant Navy and jumped ship in 1952, young white musicians have kept crossing the Atlantic to learn the craft at first-hand.

The truth is that nowadays, with dancers clamouring for the newer kinds of pop, with the goings-on at Preservation and Dixieland Halls appealing strictly to the tourists, it is only the marching bands—used for ordinary parades, of course, as well as for funerals—that play a genuine role in Negro social life. They alone seem to be keeping New Orleans music alive.

Left *Louis Armstrong, New Orleans' most celebrated son, symbolized the ethos of jazz. The first great jazz soloist, he changed the sound and style of every sort of trumpeter. His Hot Five and Hot Seven records of the 1920s were to be jazz classics. In the 1930s he became internationally famous, touring Europe, making films, and the following decades found him winning the affection of millions who knew nothing about jazz technicalities but could recognize a unique human being. His death, aged 71, in the summer of 1971, stunned jazz fans throughout the world. Teen-agers in New York (below), where Armstrong was buried, demonstrate how Satchmo spanned the generations, while in New Orleans all the bands paraded in his honour.*

# Mainstream Men

England is sometimes thought of as the home of compromise. So there may be a shred of poetic justice in the fact that an English jazz critic, Stanley Dance, dreamed up the term 'mainstream'—even if he did settle down in the United States only a year or two later. What Dance sought was a word to describe the kind of jazz closest to his heart, that musical plateau lying between New Orleans and bebop, bordered at one end by Jelly Roll Morton's Red Hot Peppers, at the other by Charlie Parker and the men from Minton's. There was no suggestion that mainstream might be an identifiable style of playing, apart from the fact that the majority of performers came of musical age just as ensemble skills were becoming unfashionable, when the solo seemed an end in itself. Nor does mainstream fit tidily inside a precise period, for although the players mostly flourished during the 1930s they were joined later on by younger men, many not even born when Coleman Hawkins discovered a way of playing jazz on the saxophone, or Roy Eldridge acted as link-man between Louis Armstrong and Dizzy Gillespie.

Stanley Dance coined the term towards the end of the 1950s, at a moment when the music itself was either being scoffed at by the smarter modernists or condemned as deviationist by New Orleans purists. Even musicians as dazzling as Ben Webster and Coleman Hawkins found the going tough. But being out of fashion is a strictly temporal condition, as impermanent as it is predictable, and the 1960s saw the mainstreamers make their comeback. Anyway, not all of them had suffered neglect. Louis Armstrong for one.

Armstrong may not be everybody's idea of a mainstreamer, yet more than any other man he invented the notion of the jazz soloist. At the start of the

1920s he was playing second cornet in King Oliver's Creole Jazz Band, that nonpareil of New Orleans ensembles. Yet within a couple of years Armstrong was asserting the rights of the gifted individual, laying down a grammar for jazz improvisation, showing how solos could be more than simple embellishment or arpeggiation. No musician active in the 1920s or 1930s, whatever his instrument, remained untouched by Armstrong's influence. To call any jazz player a genius invites quibbling, but Armstrong was one of the exceptions. Even in his last years, when he needed to nurse his lip, when he tended to sing much more than blow, Louis Armstrong could still unleash trumpet solos that were majestic, almost Miltonic. And on a popular level he remained a phenomenon. If *Mack The Knife* and *Hello, Dolly* lacked the staying-power of *West End Blues* and *Knockin' A Jug*, they did reflect the man's extraordinary zest for living as well as his immense professionalism.

Benny Goodman may never have got within cutting distance of Louis Armstrong as a jazz player, but in his heyday he was every bit as famous.

A genuine virtuoso of the clarinet, leader of the first successful swing band, a man who changed American musical taste, Goodman also cocked a snook at the colour bar by hiring the black musicians, Teddy Wilson and Lionel Hampton, both still around and playing very much as they used to. He even helped swing to escalate into bebop by taking on a young electric guitarist, Charlie Christian, who in his off-hours jammed at small Harlem clubs alongside Thelonious Monk, Kenny Clarke and Dizzy Gillespie. But Goodman's loyalties were divided. In 1938, at the height of his popularity, he made his first classical recording, playing Mozart's Quintet, K.581, with the Budapest String Quartet. Nowadays, even though he occasionally gets a band together for a tour, Benny Goodman is much more likely to be found performing Brahms at the Amsterdam Concertgebouw than blowing chorus after chorus of *Avalon*.

Like plenty of other white Chicago musicians anxious to better themselves, Goodman had moved to New York by the start of the 1930s. It was a bunch of those players (Goodman, as it happens, was not among them) which

Left *Two generations of mainstreamers. Veteran alto saxophonist, bandleader and composer, Benny Carter, with Ruby Braff (cornet).* Right *Louis Armstrong flanked by two of his All Stars: Tyree Glenn (trombone) and Eddie Shu (clarinet).*

formed one of the intenser coteries of pre-war jazz, a shining example of musical camaraderie. At its centre was the self-appointed leader and publicist, Eddie Condon, part-time guitarist, cynical idealist, non-stop wisecracker ('They flat their fifths, we drink ours' was his definition of bebop). Later on Condon opened his own club, but at the end of the 1930s and for some years to come the action was mostly at Nick's, in Greenwich Village, full of stuffed birds in glass cases, with moth-eaten moose heads on the walls and a proprietor, Nick Rongetti, who insisted on taking a piano solo at least once a night. But not every member of this coterie had a Chicago birth-certificate. The clarinettist Pee Wee Russell, once acclaimed by Kingsley Amis as 'the greatest poet since W. B. Yeats', grew up in St Louis, while Max Kaminsky, a trumpeter able to lead a band with the sort of passion other men pour into solos, was born on the edge of Boston. Some of those musicians are dead; others—Bobby Hackett, for example, once touted as a second Bix—have strayed into bordering territory. Among those still soldiering on is Bud Freeman, equally famous for his elliptical way of playing the tenor saxophone, and his addiction to English tweeds and English mores.

Although Benny Goodman's orchestra sold more records and pulled in huger crowds than any of its rivals, bands like Duke Ellington's and Count Basie's possessed greater quiddity. They also contained—and still contain—some of the best musicians in jazz. Johnny Hodges, Cootie Williams and Ben Webster are just three who have been both major voices in Ellington's music and important soloists in their own right. Count Basie's orchestra boasted the best pre-war rhythm section, made up of Basie (piano), Freddie Green (guitar), Walter Page (bass) and Jo Jones (drums), while its roster of soloists included the late Lester Young, another musician who pointed the way to modern jazz, as well as trumpeters Buck Clayton and Harry Edison, trombonists Dickie Wells, Bennie Morton and Vic Dickenson, and saxophonists Earl Warren and Buddy Tate—most of them still hard at work today.

During the bleaker years—the 1950s and early 1960s—quite a few main-streamers earned good money with Norman Granz's 'Jazz At The Philharmonic', touring the theatres and concert halls of Europe and America, helping to demonstrate Granz's theory that mixing musicians produced the best jazz. None of JATP's successors has operated on quite the same scale, although 'Jazz From A Swinging Era' featured plenty of Basie sidemen, together with Roy Eldridge and Earl Hines. In the 1920s Hines revolutionized the craft of jazz piano playing, and

Top *Lionel Hampton, the first great vibraphonist.* Middle *Trumpeter Buck Clayton, a star of the pre-war Count Basie Orchestra.* Bottom *Earl Hines, a giant rediscovered.* Right *Benny Goodman, one-time King of Swing.*

made classic records with Louis Armstrong, then led his own big band (in 1943 he even had Dizzy Gillespie and Charlie Parker working for him). The fact that Hines operated in near-obscurity for over a decade only being rediscovered in the 1960s, shows that even one of the greatest jazz musicians could be sidetracked by fashion.

More recently, George Wein's Newport All Stars—named after the festival on Rhode Island but actually touring all over Europe—mopped up a lot of mainstream talent. It was Wein who persuaded Benny Carter, a star musician and arranger of the 1930s, to desert his film and TV writing for a while and fashion more of the creamy, elegant solos for which he used to be famous. Other old-timers who play for Wein include Red Norvo and Joe Venuti, both of whom once worked in Paul Whiteman's orchestra. Since those far-off days Norvo has led one of the discreetest swing bands of the 1930s and switched from xylophone to vibraphone without injuring his cool, crisp style, while Venuti, notorious for his practical jokes—he once chewed Whiteman's violin to pieces on-stage—is a gustier jazz violinist than when he recorded those 40-year-old duets with the guitarist Eddie Lang.

But these are all men with a past, their careers stretching back to the years between the wars. Of the younger Americans who have opted for an older tradition, the best-known is Ruby Braff, a cornet player with a plummy tone, a dainty way of phrasing, sounding a bit like Louis or Bix glimpsed through rose-tinted spectacles. Not surprisingly, Britons are well represented. Alex Welsh leads a band that contains two exceptional soloists in the trombonist Roy Williams and the baritone saxophonist Johnny Barnes. There is the Scottish clarinettist Sandy Brown, actually earning his living as an acoustics engineer; the alto saxophonist Bruce Turner, who once studied with Lennie Tristano and can, when he chooses to, sound like 1949-vintage Lee Konitz, but whose long-term heroes are Pete Brown and Johnny Hodges; and Humphrey Lyttelton, ex-Etonian, ex-Guards officer, ex-New Orleans revivalist, whose career as a trumpeter and bandleader almost retraces the history of jazz. None of these men were around when Ben Webster, Lester Young and Dick Wilson tried to cut Coleman Hawkins in Kansas City, nor when Jack Teagarden headed for Harlem to jam with Fats Waller and Jimmy Harrison. But their aesthetic instinct led them to the easy-going kind of jazz, with plenty of solos and—most of the time, anyway—pre-Parker harmonies, that Stanley Dance was thinking of when he coined his new category.

Left *Cootie Williams, featured soloist with Duke Ellington.* Above *Roy Eldridge, link-man between Louis Armstrong and Dizzy Gillespie.* Right *Chicago tenor saxophonist, Bud Freeman.*

# Modernists

The image the jazz musician presents to the world and the image he carries inside his head have gone through more than a sea-change since the First World War. In the New Orleans of Buddy Bolden and Freddy Keppard the musician could have been the man next door, doing a daytime job yet also dressing up regularly to march in parades, or hurrying off to play at a picnic or a local dance. As jazz caught on in other parts of America its function narrowed; in Chicago and New York, for example, the music had fewer social roots but even more entertainment value. So jazz became an enclave of show business, restricted to theatres and ballrooms and clubs, mostly used for dancing or drinking or making whoopee to. By 1932 Louis Armstrong's reputation had spread far enough for the trumpeter to have been booked into the London Palladium, yet most people thought of him not as a superb improviser, the soloist of *West End Blues* and *Muggles,* but as a gritty-voiced entertainer, adept at skewering one high C after another. Pleasing the paying customer had become a discipline that musicians ignored only if they were prepared to start missing meals. Those who matured during the 1920s and 1930s accepted the situation unthinkingly, yet the best of them—men like Coleman Hawkins, Duke Ellington, Earl Hines—had the built-in cunning of the natural artist, the ability to please themselves while pleasing their audiences.

In the 1940s the beboppers wrought changes that were psychological as well as musical and sprang from a variety of discontents. Among these was that impatience the young always feel for their elders, the need to mock and if possible outdo the middle-aged. Another was the second-class status of the jazz musician and America's failure to accredit him as an artist. Then there was the chagrin felt by black men who had just seen white men cashing in on music they felt was theirs. For although the black neighbourhoods and the jazz buffs knew that Duke Ellington and Count Basie and Jimmie Lunceford led the best big bands, the vast American public had different ideas, showering its admiration and its dollars on Benny Goodman, Tommy Dorsey and Artie Shaw. Finally there was the aesthetic problem, the fact that the wellworn harmonies, rhythms and riffs of the swing era gave a new generation of players no chance to flex their muscles.

Some of the answers got worked out at after-hours jam sessions in Clark Monroe's Uptown House, Minton's Playhouse and other Harlem clubs. Most of the musicians taking part were young, obscure, still on the way up; men like Charlie Parker, fresh out of Kansas City, Dizzy Gillespie from Cab Calloway's orchestra, the drummer Kenny Clarke and pianists Bud Powell and Thelonious Monk. What they did was to complicate the chords and rhythms, to make the music at once harder to play yet also capable of expressing more. The psychological change was important too. For the first time the jazz musician began thinking of himself as an artist; a few even celebrated this emancipation by playing with their backs to the audience. Social mores were affected as well. Dandyism had always been a facet of black American culture, but now beboppers dressed to emphasize their apartness from the crewcut world, developing an argot only the hip could understand. It was partly a gesture of nonconformism, partly showmanship—like Dizzy Gillespie's beret, hornrimmed glasses and goatee beard. Another innovation was not so trivial. Instead of hitting the bottle or puffing on a reefer, traditional ways in which jazzmen had relaxed, there was a cult of heroin and the needle. Charlie Parker, Fats Navarro, Wardell Gray, Bud Powell and too many others died either directly or indirectly from drugs. And there were unfamiliar political and religious tremors. Twenty years before Cassius Clay turned into Muhammad Ali some jazz musicians were embracing Islam. The saxophonists Edmund Gregory and William Evans became Sahib Shihab and Yusef Lateef; even the drummer Art Blakey started calling himself Abdullah Ibn Buhaina.

*Dizzy Gillespie with his custom-built trumpet, partnered by the saxophonist and flautist James Moody.*

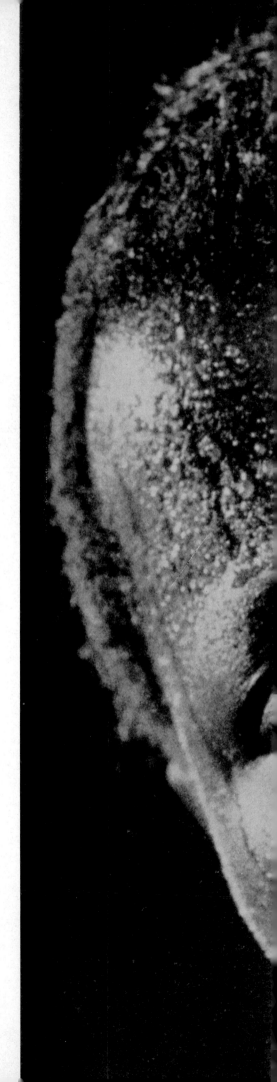

Left *Alto saxophonist Lee Konitz, who began as a disciple of Lennie Tristano.* Right *Canadian-born Oscar Peterson, a jazz pianist whose virtuosity pulls in the crowds.*

Africa intruded in other ways too. The black writer, Leroi Jones, in his book *Blues People*, points out how both bebop tunes and African melodies have often been extensions of rhythmic figures, sometimes complete with onomatopoeic titles like *Oo-po-a-da,* even 'bebop' itself. Yet the beboppers also complicated the chord sequences, edging closer to Europe where 19th-century composers had pursued harmony almost for its own sake. And just as the end of the 1920s found New York session men like Red Nichols, Miff Mole and Eddie Lang— all white, all brimming with technical know-how—tidying jazz up, replacing the fervent with the formal, so history repeated itself in the 1950s. This time the action mostly took place on the West Coast, the work of a coterie of white musicians attracted by the TV, film and recording studios in Los Angeles. It was there that Gerry Mulligan dropped the piano from his line-up, forming a quartet which cultivated a dry counterpoint, a witty, conversational style. It was there that Dave Brubeck paraded round the college circuit, juggling with tricky time-signatures, convincing earnest young Americans that jazz was serious enough to be listened to sitting down.

Coolness was nothing new. As far back as the 1920s, Frankie Trumbauer's solos on C-melody sax sounded

decidedly aloof, especially when heard alongside Bix Beiderbecke's gustier cornet. But the cult of under-statement really began when Lester Young arrived in New York with Count Basie's orchestra in 1936. It was strengthened by the nine-piece band Miles Davis got together twelve years later, which appeared in public only a handful of times—at the Royal Roost, a chicken restaurant on Broadway—but recorded a set of 78s that brought a new ambience to small-group jazz. Lester Young's influence was largely second-hand, exerted through the bevy of young saxophonists who adopted his laconic style as a starting-point, most of them white, like Stan Getz, whose turtle-dove tone and dainty phrasing summed up the situation. As for Miles Davis, it was not so much his trumpet playing which sparked off the trend but the efforts of his arrangers—Gerry Mulligan, Gil Evans and, most significantly, John Lewis, who within a few years was using the Modern Jazz Quartet as the vehicle for a cultural get-together, yoking the twelve-bar blues to Renaissance forms and functions. Counterpoint, but minus the rococo trimmings, was also cherished by the white pianist Lennie Tristano, almost as famous for teaching as for playing, the leader of a quintet that included the alto saxophonist Lee Konitz.

Beboppers, of course, had not been alone in deriding the swing bands. Other musicians every bit as young and idealistic, but nearly all white, thought salvation lay in revisiting the past. To them New Orleans at the start of the century seemed like Eden before the Fall. Similarly, when the prissiness and over-formality of much 1950s jazz produced a reaction, this once again split two ways. The new innovators, men like Ornette Coleman and Cecil Taylor, set about making radical changes. Others preferred to look behind them, if sometimes only for very short distances. For example, Art Blakey's Jazz Messengers specialized in hard bop, a tight, crackling style that revamped the original precepts of Gillespie and Parker. Older black musicians were usually reluctant to delve back even as far as that. If the average sideman of the 1930s thought about early jazz, it was patronisingly; as for worksongs and country blues, they seemed too close to slavery for comfort. But in 1960, while black had not yet become officially beautiful, American Negroes were already taking pride in their culture. Blues and gospel

music had always been popular at grassroots level; now they began to be reflected—stylized, often dressed up as 'funk' and 'soul'—in the jazz of Cannonball Adderley, Horace Silver and—most massively, most creatively—Charles Mingus.

But these shifts in taste did not mean the bulk of musicians changed their styles to order, even if shallower talents were disposed to do so. The essence of jazz lies in identity, the way a performer of quality remains unmistakably himself. A few—Miles Davis for one, Sonny Rollins for another—contrive to do this while continuing to evolve, driven by outsize aesthetic curiosity and a distaste for repeating themselves. The vast majority, including the three great originators, Louis Armstrong, Charlie Parker and Ornette Coleman, have discovered their musical identities, and afterwards stayed substantially the same. Within a decade an iconoclast can be transformed into an Establishment figure, his principles uncompromised, his methods undiluted. It happened to the men who gathered at Minton's just as it happens to revolutionaries after every flashpoint in history.

Top left *Dave Brubeck with Jack Six (bass)*. Left *Max Roach at the 1967 Newport Jazz Festival*. Above *Gerry Mulligan*. Right *An architect of bebop, pianist-composer Thelonious Monk*.

22

Left *Stan Getz, a soloist with a turtle-dove tone.* Below *Alto saxophonist Jackie McLean, featured with Charles Mingus and Art Blakey.* Right *Sonny Rollins.*

Left *The Modern Jazz Quartet: Milt Jackson (vibraphone), Connie Kay (drums), Percy Heath (bass), John Lewis (piano). Kay replaced Kenny Clarke in 1955; the other three have been together since 1952.* Below *Milt Jackson, known to his friends as 'Bags'.*

# Jazz Composers

Gambler, braggart, con-man, bordello pianist—Jelly Roll Morton was all these things. In addition, he happened to be the first jazz composer, giving the music a formality which contrasted with the maelstrom of his life-style. But Morton's cocksureness, however much it infuriated his contemporaries, may have been an artistic advantage, for what he really did was to impose himself upon the New Orleans ensemble, harnessing the traditional front-line—trumpet, clarinet, trombone—to his own ends. The musicians still improvised, but under orders. Some have recalled how, before a recording session, Morton would sit at the piano, playing a phrase or two, indicating the kind of effects he wanted. For Morton was no mere tune-writer—he did that as well, and lavishly—but a composer who thought in terms of a total sound, an overall pattern. He had started out as a ragtime pianist in the red-light district of New Orleans. Ragtime, in fact, seems to have been a regular training ground for the first jazz composers. Duke Ellington, fourteen years younger than Morton, played it in the early 1920s at Harlem 'house rent' parties. And if Morton was the Mozart of jazz, Ellington has been its Beethoven, unabashedly romantic. He, too, built his strategy around soloists, but presented them in dramatic settings or against sensuous textures. He learned his orchestration on the job, writing scores to fit behind dance-routines at the Cotton Club, making aesthetic capital out of the demand for night-club exotica, those growls and raspings and wheezings that smart New Yorkers imagined came straight out of the jungle.

Jelly Roll died in 1941, hard-up, convinced a voodoo curse had dragged him down. Somebody even stole the diamond from his front tooth while he lay in his coffin. By then Duke Ellington was already an international celebrity, basking in a fame which still sends him off patrolling the theatres and concert halls of the world. For the point of Ellington's works—just like Morton's, just like any genuine jazz composer's—is that they need to be performed by a particular set of musicians. Only one other man had been allowed—regularly, that is—to

write for Ellington's unique ensemble; he was Billy Strayhorn, Ellington's full-time amanuensis and collaborator from 1939 until his death in 1967. Arguments are likely to go on raging about who wrote which bits of some compositions, so expertly did Strayhorn assimilate the Ellington manner, although echoes of Debussy and Ravel betray where Strayhorn did his growing up. The two men worked together on several of the suites that the Ellington orchestra played during the 1950s and 1960s, yet Ellington's pioneering of extended jazz composition stretches

Left *Duke Ellington hard at work.* Above *George Russell.*

back much further. It was in January 1929, when the band recorded *Tiger Rag,* that Ellington became the first jazzman to let a performance spill over both sides of a 78 disc. But that was very much a matter of packing in extra solos. Two years later, on 20 January 1931, something more important happened. Amateur criminologists will associate that date with a classic crime, the murder of Julia Wallace in Liverpool and the search by her husband—innocently or to set up an alibi, the alternatives still tantalize—for the non-existent Menlove Gardens East. At almost the same moment, two

thousand miles away in New York, the Duke Ellington Orchestra made jazz history by recording *Creole Rhapsody,* significant not just because it lasted for six minutes rather than three but for the way it thrust back the boundaries, conceptual as much as structural, that had hemmed jazz in until then.

If Jelly Roll Morton's compositions summed up the ethos of New Orleans collective improvising, Ellington's did the same for the virtuoso solo playing of the 1930s. When bebop surfaced in the 1940s jazz composers had to rethink their position. One of them, Tadd Dameron, not only wrote some of the most piquant of the new themes (*Hot House,* using the chords of *What Is This Thing Called Love?,* is a dazzling example), but devised backgrounds that gave perspective to the solos. He was not the only young composer to think in terms of a small group rather than a big band. Thelonious Monk's pieces, harmonically daring, their melodies as bumpy as the composer's piano solos, were planned for trios or quartets, while John Lewis, once Dizzy Gillespie's pianist, wrote for an all-percussion ensemble—vibraphone, piano, bass, drums. Wearing dinner jackets and the soberest mien of any jazzmen, the Modern Jazz Quartet spent the 1950s and 1960s treading delicately between the composed and the improvised. Importing the art of fugue into jazz was nothing new—Reginald Foresythe had done it with *Dodging A Divorcee* in 1935, three years later Benny Goodman recorded Alec Templeton's *Bach Goes To Town*—but Lewis used fugue, canon and other baroque devices regularly.

Not surprisingly, John Lewis also became active in Third Stream, Gunther Schuller's phrase for the confluence of jazz and classical musics, an hybrid Stan Kenton had already toyed with. Kenton's orchestra mixed Wagnerian bombast with more thoughtful scores, including some by Bill Russo, who stayed faithful to the genre until the end of the 1960s, when he opted for guitars, spontaneity and a Rock Cantata. George Russell was another composer who dipped into Third Stream and later deserted it, preferring a looser approach and the stimulus of adventuring soloists. Russell had drummed in Benny Carter's band, written the first Afro-Cuban scores for Dizzy Gillespie, and formulated his own musical theory, the Lydian Concept of Tonal Organization.

Texture, the sophistication of harmony, always fascinated Duke Ellington, just as it did his contemporary, Don Redman. It became virtually the *raison d'être* of Gil Evans's work. A Canadian who wrote arrangements for Claude Thornhill's Orchestra, one of the best commercial dance bands of the 1940s, and after that for Miles Davis, Gil Evans is fascinated by sounds. ('When I was a kid,' he told the American jazz critic Nat Hentoff, 'I could tell what kind of car was coming with my back turned.') The scores he wrote for Miles Davis during

the 1950s were the plushest ever heard in jazz, although achieving richness economically, with a minimum of instruments. Evans was unusual in preferring to decorate other mens' themes instead of writing fresh ones, not so much arranging as recomposing them, turning Gershwin or Kurt Weill tunes into his own artistic property. And at a time when intricacy often just meant sounding busy, Evans's orchestrations hung like heavy tapestries, undulating rather than moving, given rhythmic life by the soloists who flared across them.

Rhythmic vitality, on the other hand, lies at the heart of Charles Mingus's music. Possibly the greatest jazz composer since Duke Ellington, a virtuoso bassist who has worked with Kid Ory and Louis Armstrong, with the Ellington and Lionel Hampton

orchestras, with Charlie Parker and Bud Powell, Mingus is much possessed by time, not as a scavenger of odd time-signatures but more functionally. In his bands the rhythm section rarely stays separate from the front-line; instead there is a weaving in and out, bass and drums playing tunes, trumpets and saxophones suggesting rhythms. His music is packed with allusions, to Fats Waller, Lester Young, Duke Ellington's way with saxophones, the quicksilver dartings of bebop, yet the curving, slow-motion tunes and built-in gospel fervour reflect the man, sensual and passionate. Mingus leads his bands from behind the bass rather like a military commander directing a sortie, suiting his tactics to the mood or needs of the moment. The listener can take nothing for granted. A familiar composition may suddenly alter course, assume a completely new identity.

If Charles Mingus is the most recent jazz composer to be generally looked on as major, the 1960s have seen plenty of other composers and arrangers evolve or decline or simply stay around the scene: Bill Dixon, Clare Fischer, Oliver Nelson, Quincy Jones, Benny Golson, Tom McIntosh, Mike Mantler, Don Sebesky, even a woman, Carla Bley. At one time the wife of the Canadian pianist, Paul Bley, she started by writing spare but intriguing themes, then developed a composing style which takes in irony and satire. Mrs Bley's scores for Charlie Haden's Liberation Music and 'A Genuine Tong Funeral' (recorded by Gary Burton) alternate between sounding like the music for a Brecht play, *circa* 1930, and one of Mingus's zanier outings. But eclecticism is as commonplace in present-day jazz as in pop. The British composer Mike Westbrook jumbles together periods and styles and media (he has thrown in lantern slides, all-in wrestling, even razor-blade swallowing), adopting what could be called a humanist standpoint, never afraid—just like Duke Ellington—of appearing sentimental, and letting his soloists take a good deal of the glory. At the opposite extreme are two other Britons, Howard Riley and Barry Guy, both members of Riley's Trio (Guy is an exceptionally talented bassist), both classically trained composers, whose jazz pieces are sometimes chilly but also terse and dry, like a good Norman Calvados.

Perhaps the British have more of a taste for paradox than most people, which may be why jazz composers abound among them. There is Stan Tracey, with his gift for lyrical

*Two jazz composers in action.* Left *Charles Mingus leads from behind his double bass.* Right *John Lewis at the piano.*

melancholy, his way of making saxophones take on a new persona; Graham Collier, who, rather like George Russell, has moved from writing tautly, with every note planned, to a situation where the musicians have freedom yet the composer still keeps the whip-hand; Neil Ardley, who also runs the New Jazz Orchestra; Kenny Wheeler, as modest about his composing as about his felicitous brass playing; and Michael Garrick, whose liturgical pieces—he uses a choir as well as jazz soloists—have echoed around the dome of St Paul's Cathedral. The twelve-tone method has been applied by David Mack, who even had the trumpeter Shake Keane improvising serially, and—in his most recent phase—by the veteran, John Dankworth. Keith Tippett, from the West Country, straddles pop and jazz, while Mike Taylor wrote songs for The Cream as well as deliciously original jazz themes before his body was found floating in the sea. Another composer with a foot in rock as well as jazz is Mike Gibbs: a Rhodesian living in London, constantly plagued by Stan Getz and Garry Burton to write pieces for them, Gibbs has evolved a big band style as ambrosial as marzipan but able to yelp like vintage Herman.

Several of these men have received bursaries from the Arts Council of Great Britain; all are articulate, aware of what they are doing. None, at a first glance, would seem to have much in common with the brash-talking Jelly Roll Morton, 'that old whore-house pianist', as W. C. Handy once called him. Yet, consciously or un-consciously, they have inherited precepts that Morton put on record nearly half a century ago, his recipe for keeping a firm grip on events in general while writing with particular musicians in mind. Perhaps Duke Ellington, a great trader in adages, has put it most neatly, and in a form Jelly Roll might have used himself. 'Every musician has his favourite licks and you gotta write to them,' Duke assured a fellow-passenger during the railroad journey from Cleveland to Pittsburgh. 'I guess you can't compose music right unless you know how the man that'll play it plays poker.'

Top left *Mike Westbrook, Devonshire-born bandleader and dabbler in mixed media.* Top right *Carla Bley, a composer with both a rare melodic instinct and a penchant for sharpness and satire.* Right *Graham Collier leading his band at a concert for pupils at Dagenham Girls Primary School.* Far right *Charles Mingus confronted by a non-musical problem.*

# New Innovators

Progress is the superstition of a scientific age, hubris in yet another guise but with the same built-in comeuppance, the source of those notions about bigger meaning better and the upward path leading to complexity. Between the wars plenty of jazzmen—critics and fans as well as players—fell for this package of nostrums, spurred on by knowing their music was still despised, agog to see it become respectable. As a result, the big band scores of Duke Ellington and Don Redman, the more florid improvisings of Coleman Hawkins and Art Tatum, were admired not just for their own sakes but as symbols of a sophistication that—or so everybody hoped—would give jazz harmonic parity with European music. Thinking of that sort did not collapse with the 1930s. Beboppers kowtowed to Stravinsky, Debussy, Ravel. Charlie Parker was even flattered to be asked to record with strings. Stan Kenton presented the *Concerto To End All Concertos*. As for the 1950s, they were the heydays of Third Stream, when jazz got squeezed into a classical waistcoat and Dave Brubeck wowed the campuses with *Blue Rondo A La Turk* in 9/8 time. Which made what happened next seem even more of a shock. For jazz remembered where it had come from. The black tradition reasserted itself, opting for rhythm and melody—African priorities, in fact—rather than old-style European harmony.

The man mostly responsible for the change was Ornette Coleman, 28 years old at the time—quite elderly for a jazz innovator—and, like Louis Armstrong and Charlie Parker, very largely self-taught. Just as Armstrong hailed from New Orleans and Parker from Kansas City, Coleman also grew up in blues territory—in Texas. As a teenager, zoot-suited, his hair 'conked' to a shining flatness, he honked away on his first saxophone, imitating the r-and-b hero, Big Jay McNeely. He was 19 before he realized, listening to Lester Young, that music existed which 'didn't have a dollar sign as the only reason for doing it'.

*A gentle revolutionary: Ornette Coleman, innovator and iconoclast.*

But when Coleman left his hometown, Fort Worth, it was with the Silas Green Minstrel Show; ahead lay several years of touring with rhythm-and-blues bands. Already he had started playing what he heard inside his head, and most bandleaders hated it. One left him stranded in Los Angeles, where he spent a sizeable part of the 1950s, studying musical theory while working as a lift-boy ('I used to go up to the tenth floor, park there, and read the books'.) In the evenings he walked from Watts, the black ghetto where he lived, to the downtown clubs. Those musicians who allowed him to sit in often kept him waiting until the small hours, then jeered at what he played. Dexter Gordon even refused to have him on the stand.

Not that free jazz lacked a precedent. In 1949, Lennie Tristano, with a group of his cohorts, made the first atonal jazz record—no theme, no chords, no time-signature. Yet that was an isolated experiment, done out of curiosity rather than to trigger off anything. Ornette Coleman's intentions were both more serious and more deeply felt. And however audacious his playing might have seemed at a first hearing, its roots lay in the past, not too distant from the melisma of the blues singer, the rhythmic compactness of the work-song. Chorus-lengths were ignored, themes developed for just as long as the musicians wished, yet the fact that a soloist could now play almost anything he wanted also meant that more decisions had to be taken. ('It was when I found out I could make mistakes that I knew I was on to something,' Coleman remarked much later.) A strain was put upon the inventiveness of any but the boldest, those who, like Coleman, knew more or less instinctively what worked and what did not.

'Well, I guess I'm out of date now,' said a member of the Art Farmer-Benny Golson Jazztet, the group sharing the billing at the Five Spot on that chilly autumn evening in 1959 when the Ornette Coleman Quartet faced a New York audience for the first time. Sceptics gazed suspiciously at Coleman's white plastic alto saxophone and Don Cherry's pocket Pakistani trumpet. But what upset them most,

even more than the absence of chords, were the actual sounds, especially Coleman's stinging, aggressive tone. (History was repeating itself, for the same criticism had been levelled at Charlie Parker fifteen years earlier.) But if some musicians were angry or cynical, a few were quick to praise. John Lewis had already described Coleman's music as 'the first extension of Charlie Parker I've heard,' Gunther Schuller talked about its 'deep inner logic', the composer Virgil Thomson found it the most stimulating jazz since Louis Armstrong.

Sides began to be taken, not just over Ornette Coleman but John Coltrane too. 'Anti-jazz' was one hostile critic's summing-up of an half-hour-long solo in which Coltrane permutated almost every implication of a couple of chords. Yet Coltrane's approach was almost the exact opposite of Coleman's, inhabiting a modal universe, with every note justifiable. It sprang from hearing what Coleman Hawkins did with arpeggios, especially in his classic 1939 recording of *Body and Soul*. A man almost totally dedicated to music—his only hobby was peering through a telescope in the backyard of his home in Jamaica, Long Island—Coltrane became more and more obsessed by the chord as the 1950s rolled past. The American critic, Ira Gitler, credited him with playing 'sheets of sound', a colourful phrase intended to describe the saxophonist's fondness for running through the scales suggested by each chord, yet so rapidly that they seemed continuous, even vertical. Fittingly enough, Coltrane was a member of the Miles Davis Sextet which recorded *Kind of Blue*, an LP that changed the habits of jazz improvisers all round the world. And by the time Ornette Coleman arrived at the Five Spot, Coltrane was almost ready to venture out on his own.

While musicians often remained wary of Coleman's playing they usually accepted Coltrane's innovations, partly because these seemed more explicable, extending techniques with which they were familiar, partly because of the saxophonist's earlier reputation as an orthodox jazz player. But just like Coleman, Coltrane had served his time in rhythm-and-blues bands,

Top left *Cecil Taylor*. Top right *Eric Dolphy, flautist, alto saxophonist and pioneer of the bass clarinet, who worked with Charles Mingus and John Coltrane*. Far right *John Coltrane*. Middle *Don Cherry*. Bottom *Elvin Jones*.

working with Daisey May and The Hep Cats as well as with Dizzy Gillespie and Miles Davis. Yet the music he made with his Quartet seemed far-removed from that background, almost Oriental in its concern with space. Coltrane would explore a scale every bit as exhaustively as a sitar or sarod player improvises on a raga, the tamboura's drone got implied in what the bassist and pianist were up to, while Elvin Jones, as inventive as a first-rate tabla player, built up a network of rhythms underneath. The effect could be hypnotic, a bit like watching three-dimensional chess. But there was no standing still. By the time he died—in 1967, aged only 40—Coltrane had changed his surroundings, working alongside expressionists like the tenor saxophonist Pharoah Sanders, yet without compromising the severe logic of his own playing.

Most up-and-coming young musicians still reflect the influence of either Coleman or Coltrane, sometimes both, but only a handful have got round to Cecil Taylor. Which seems unfair to a musician who made his breakthrough even earlier than the other two yet who still finds himself struggling. (When the photographer-writer, Valerie Wilmer, called on Taylor a couple of years ago he was trim and elegantly suited, but living—surrounded by empty coffee cups, odd socks and books of poetry—between two dingy warehouses in downtown Manhattan.) While Ornette Coleman worked his lift in Los Angeles and Coltrane toured with Earl Bostic and Johnny Hodges, Taylor washed dishes, sold records, delivered sandwiches, only occasionally getting paid for sitting down and playing the piano. It was not for want of an academic background. Swayed by an offhand remark of Duke Ellington's ('You need the conservatory—with an ear for what is happening in the streets'), Taylor enrolled at Boston's New England Conservatory of Music, absorbing the sounds and methods of Schoenberg, Webern, Ives and Cage. But the second half of Ellington's credo has now taken on even more significance, for Taylor regards himself as first and foremost a performer in the black tradition. 'I try to imitate on the piano the leaps in space that a dancer makes,' he once said, almost certainly having James Brown in mind rather than Nureyev.

Although Taylor generally operates with a quartet or trio, he could just as

profitably be on his own. A musician who thinks orchestrally, he is one of the most self-contained pianists in jazz, very decidedly of the same lineage as James P. Johnson and Thelonious Monk, as well as a virtuoso comparable with Bud Powell at his dizziest, or even with that nonpareil of technicians, Art Tatum. But where those musicians excelled inside an accepted manner, Taylor has created his own context, dislocating harmony almost to a condition of atonality, yet with a composer's instinct for form. Everything hangs together, although the listener often has to search hard for the key. It can usually be found in Taylor's left hand, for however ferocious the treble flurries, however intent the pianist seems on building layer after layer of sound, a figure in the bass hints at where the music is heading, exactly as it did or does in the vastly different playing of James P. and Fats Waller and Duke Ellington. As a boy, Taylor heard gospel singing when his family went to the neighbourhood church. His father sang half-remembered shouts and field hollers round the home. For Cecil Taylor, just as for Ornette Coleman and John Coltrane, the blues were a fact of everyday life and his music goes on proving it.

# Jazz in Europe

Jazz stopped being black sometime before the First World War. And scarcely had Buddy Bolden breathed his last—in East Louisiana State Hospital in November 1931—than it ceased being exclusively American too. Django Reinhardt and the serious-minded young Scot, George Chisholm, may have been lonely harbingers but they were genuinely European, jazz musicians with an identity of their own. Otherwise everybody copied the Americans, beginning with the Original Dixieland Jazz Band, who appeared in 'Joy Bells' at the London Hippodrome for just one night, 7 April 1919—the revue's star, George Robey, threatened to walk out if the Dixielanders stayed on the bill—before taking London by storm at the Palladium and the Hammersmith Palais. A dozen years later Louis Armstrong started local trumpeters searching for high C's, while Spike Hughes's band recorded compositions by their leader that genuflected before Duke Ellington, mixing Irish poteen with Harlem hooch. In between, British dance band musicians had a crush on the white New Yorkers, egged on by the Spanish-American composer, Fred Elizalde, who imported Adrian Rollini, Fud Livingston and Chelsea Quealey for the band he took into the Savoy Hotel. (Elizalde had previously led an undergraduate band at Cambridge which included M. J. C. Allom, later President of M.C.C. and the only jazz or dance band player to take a hat-trick in a Test match.) But the first truly original jazz to come out of Europe was performed by an all-string group—violin, three guitars, bass—with a name as quaint as its instrumentation: the Quintet of the Hot Club of France. Stephane Grappelly was the violinist, dazzling but overshadowed by the wizardly guitarist Django Reinhardt, full of gypsy flamboyance and *morbidezza*, his blues closer to the Camargue than the Mississippi Delta.

The arrival of George Chisholm, his trombone playing bluff, vibrant with Glasgow's equivalent of 'soul', almost coincided with the start of the Second World War and Britain's isolation from the Continent. In Nazi-occupied Europe, jazz was often a clandestine affair, harmless-sounding French or Dutch titles masking themes by banned Jewish or Negro composers. Britain saw jazz played in all sorts of unlikely surroundings, from Army Nissen huts to sandbagged Mayfair night clubs. (The blind pianist, George Shearing, was one of many musicians who worked in London throughout the Blitz.) Once the war was over, Europeans were eager to catch up. Since 1939, however, jazz had divided into two camps: revivalists gazed over their shoulders at New Orleans in its heyday, using an improvising front-line of trumpet, clarinet, trombone; modernists tiptoed in the footsteps of Charlie Parker and Dizzy Gillespie. Both types of jazz took root most deeply in the industrialized countries—France, Belgium, Holland, Germany, Britain and the Scandinavian bloc—possibly because their local folk-cultures had

Below *Tubby Hayes, a soloist who also composes, conducting his Big Band.* Right *Alto saxophonist Zbigniew Namyslowski, leader of the Polish Modern Jazz Quartet.*

decayed and young musicians needed a substitute. (It was noticeable how slowly jazz progressed in Spain, Greece and southern Italy, where folk-music was very much alive, still absorbing enthusiasm and talent.) All that European jazzmen really needed, in fact, was a sense of tradition, a chance to rub against one another, a way of learning which was not just a matter of winding up the gramophone and putting on another 78. But the next twenty years took care of that.

Sweden stayed neutral throughout the war, emerging in a healthier physical and economic condition than most other European nations. It also produced the first post-war jazz musicians capable of matching the Americans. (One of them, Stan Hasselgard, not only updated Benny Goodman's clarinet style but actually worked for a time in Goodman's orchestra until he died in a car crash in 1948.) The formality of Swedish jazz was also an advantage: musicians like the baritone saxophonist Lars Gullin, the alto saxophonist Arne Domnerus and the pianist Bengt Hallberg found themselves very much in tune with American 'cool' jazz of the 1950s. Norway, shorter of talent, had a good trumpeter in Rowland Greenberg, as well as the tenor saxophonist Bjarne Nerem. In Denmark the violinist Svend Asmussen maintained his pre-war brilliance while Niels Henning Orsted-Pedersen has proved himself one of the world's finest bass players.

Jim Europe's Hell-Fighters, the all-black band of the American 369th Infantry Division, featuring rags quite as often as marches, gave France its first taste of jazz in 1917. By 1928 Jean Cocteau was taking jazz as seriously as poetry or painting, helping to create an aesthetic climate which proved salutary for Django Reinhardt, Stephane Grappelly and the younger musicians who joined in after the war. Some were highly original, like the pianist Martial Solal and, more recently, Jean-Luc Ponty, the first man to make a real success of playing modern jazz on the violin. Even Sacha Distel's guitar was heard on records by John Lewis and other Americans before his romantic image took over. Belgium

has produced a handful of good jazz musicians—the vibraphonist Fats Sadi, the flautist Bobby Jaspar, the guitarist René Thomas—but most have hurried off to work in Paris. Holland, although a haven for visiting Americans during the 1930s, had few local jazzmen until it became a centre of avant-garde irruptions thirty years later. (Some of the better Dutch free players are mentioned elsewhere in this book.) As for Switzerland, its reputation as a nation of timekeepers—Harry Lime, Orson Welles and Graham Greene share the blame for narrowing the image down to cuckoo clocks—is strengthened by the fact that one of Europe's finest drummers, Daniel Humair, grew up alongside Lake Geneva.

Not surprisingly, jazz was weakest in the two Axis partners, Italy and Germany, despite the fact that the Duce's younger son, Romano Mussolini, later blossomed out as a Shearing-style pianist. Germany's role in jazz history had been enacted entirely by proxy, for Leon Bismarck Beiderbecke, although born in Davenport, Iowa, sprang from ancestors who were clergymen and organists in Pomerania and Mecklenburg. Bix's special kind of musicality, lyrical but precise, a long way from the blues, is echoed today in the solos of Albert Mangelsdorff, an unusually gifted trombonist, while other outstanding German musicians are Karl Berger and Gunter Hampel, both vibraphone players, and—from East Germany—the brothers Rolf and Joachim Kuhn, a clarinettist and pianist respectively. Most jazz musicians reared in Austria seem to have gone else-where: the tenor saxophonist Hans Koller works in Germany; Mike Mantler, a trumpet-playing composer, and the pianist and baritone saxophonist Friedrich Gulda, better-known as an interpreter of Mozart, both live in the United States.

Just as New York once acted as a magnet for jazz musicians all over America, the West has attracted players from behind the Iron Curtain. The Hungarian vibraphonist Gabor Szabo, the Yugoslav trumpeter Dusko Gojkovic, and the Czech bassist Miroslav Vitous, are three who have proved themselves the equals of the best Americans. Colleagues left behind are sometimes cossetted, given State grants and an official status, sometimes rebuffed. The icy line taken by Stalin and his immediate successors contrasts oddly with the rapturous reception given to American jazzmen who toured the Soviet Union during the 1920s, and the fact that the first Russian jazz band, in name, if in nothing else, was started up in Leningrad as early as 1924. Yet the spirit of local nationalism which gets encouraged—in the arts, at any rate—in Eastern Europe shows its strength in the folk material used by such groups as the Polish Modern Jazz Quartet, led by the alto saxophonist Zbigniew Namyslowski, and the Zagreb Jazz Quartet, including two unique players in the bassist Miljenko Prohaska and the vibraphonist Bosko Petrovic. Even more recently, the Polish multi-instrumentalist, Michal Urbaniak—long-haired, mustachioed, with a singing wife, Urszula Dubziak—has proved himself adept on the guitar and the tenor and baritone saxophones, but is most remarkable for the jazz he coaxes out of his violin.

The quantity and quality of British jazz musicians since the 1950s is a phenomenon, not just a British critic's chauvinism. Many, like the extra-ordinary John Surman, are dealt with elsewhere, but among others deserving mention are the trumpeters Kenny Wheeler, Henry Lowther and Harold Beckett (a Barbadian with a charismatic sound); the trombonists Malcolm Griffiths, Chris Pyne and Paul Rutherford; the alto saxophonists Mike Osborne, Peter King and the Australian, Ray Warleigh; the vibraphone players Victor Feldman (he emigrated to the United States in 1955) and Frank Ricotti; the pianists Gordon Beck, John Taylor and Mike Pyne; and a clutch of tenor saxophonists: Tubby Hayes, Ronnie Scott (he also runs a club, keeps an eye on the horses and hoards antique jokes), Don Rendell, Tony Coe, Art Themen (a doctor who plays jazz in his time off), Alan Skidmore and Alan Wakeman, although perhaps the most individual and the most under-rated is a tiny Glaswegian, Bobby Wellins, who plays ballads with a haunted sound, a bit like Billie Holiday's singing. John McLaughlin and Louis Stewart (a Dubliner, not British at all) are two of the best guitarists in jazz. Even the thudding rhythm sections are disappearing, although good drummers—Phil Seamen was the first of this brand-new species—still lie thin on the ground. The really strong men are the bassists, including Jeff Clyne, Malcolm Cecil (another Briton in America), Danny Thompson, Barry Guy, Peter Ind, Ron Matthewson, Harry Miller and Chris Lawrence. But perhaps the new European is best illustrated by Dave Holland, born in Wolverhampton, who started out playing bass guitar in a rock group, The Piltdown Men, but by 1968 had moved into the Miles Davis Sextet. Only a bigot would dispute that musicians like Holland and John Surman, like Jean-Luc Ponty and Albert Mangelsdorff, rank with any in the world. Europe, in fact, is no longer a musical colony of America. The next jazz innovator could easily have a white face, and speak with the accent of Paris or Hamburg or the English shires.

*A 1960s partnership: Don Rendell and Ian Carr.*

Left *Ralf Hubner, Albert Mangelsdorff, Heinz Sauer.* Above *Han Bennink setting up his drums.* Right *French violinist Jean-Luc-Ponty.*

# Sanctified Sound

'He's singing the blues but his sound is sanctified. You know, that ain't right.' Big Bill Broonzy's outraged reaction on first hearing Ray Charles was typical of how his generation felt about the incompatability of blues and gospel. Broonzy did not demur when he toured with Mahalia Jackson and the gospel singer insisted on an interval separating her half of the concert from his sinful songs. Another old-time singer and guitarist, Son House, selected a telling verb when he declared, 'I was seduced from gospel by the sound of the blues.' What Ray Charles did towards the end of the 1950s was to bring the two worlds together, putting secular words to gospel tunes ('This little light of mine' got turned into 'This little girl of mine'), endowing blues with an ornateness of phrasing which sometimes made them seem self-pitying. Charles may not have been the only begetter of 'soul' but he was certainly in at its birth.

Not that everybody called it 'soul' to begin with. 'Funk' was the word most favoured by jazz players, derived not from Casimir Funk, the Polish biochemist who mass-produced adrenalin, nor from 'Peter Funk', the name given to a bidder who deliberately keeps prices up at an auction, but from a slang expression, meaning smell or stink, coined in seventeenth-century England yet still being bandied about in the New Orleans of Buddy Bolden's day. The musical gestures accompanying it were part of a backlash against the gentility which overcame a great deal of jazz during the 1950s. Art Blakey went into reverse, concocting an updated version of bebop. Others looked outside for inspiration, seizing upon the phrases and rhythms, frequently 3/4 and 6/8, of the music in black neighbourhood churches. This return to roots could often be self-conscious, with second-raters finding plenty of clichés to hammer out, yet a handful of musicians —Horace Silver, Cannonball Adderley's little band, above all Charles Mingus, the most creative user of the idiom—did plenty to justify this delving into the black tradition.

*Black voices, sacred words.*

Meanwhile gospel music itself was very much alive, possibly the most thriving branch on the Afro-American tree. Those versions of spirituals, harmonized to appeal to conventional European taste, that the Fisk Jubilee Singers helped to popularize during the nineteenth century, had only been a small part of the reality. The original African abrasiveness could still be found in the black churches, discernible in the call-and-response dialogue between the preacher and his congregation, in the way worshippers often became possessed, overwhelmed by fervour or intensity. It surfaced even in modern-style gospel groups, their styles influenced by the close-harmony singing of the Mills Brothers, groups like The Spirit of Memphis and The Six Blind Boys, making records, broadcasting over local radio stations, as constantly on tap for black listeners as ordinary pop music. Even the obvious theatricality and calculated bursts of hysteria were not really alien to African practices.

Other performers used more familiar methods. The Reverend Gary Davis, a blind singer and guitarist in the folk tradition, roamed the streets of Harlem. The awesome Mahalia Jackson learned her artistry in the Southern Baptist churches; as stately as Dame Clara Butt, she had the same tendency to mix banality—in her case, religioso songs like *I Believe*—with near-sublimity. There were the impassioned duets of Sister Rosetta Tharpe and Marie Knight. Sometimes straight gospel got across to the public at large. The Edwin Hawkins' Singers, whose record of *Oh Happy Day* reached the Top Twenty in 1970, was a genuine church choir from California. Seven years earlier, 'Black Nativity', an all-gospel show, had taken London audiences by storm. Yet it was somehow typical that in 1969 Madeline Bell, one of the leading singers from 'Black Nativity', should be a member of a gospel-based pop group, Blue Mink.

It reflected the way the church sound had been incorporated in black pop music. Ray Charles may have given the go-ahead but the real take-over began during the 1960s, largely through the activities of Berry Gordy, whose Tamla-Motown label, based in Detroit, was one of the few record companies to be owned by blacks. (Gordy knocked down two interior walls inside his house to make the first recording studio, still used by Motown today.) Gospel trimmings were woven into the arrangements as well as the singing, jingling tambourines and hand-clapping often forming part of the background. The Temptations and the Four Tops, with Levi Stubbs singing a high-up lead, were two of the leading male groups, and there was the slightly too glossy Diana Ross with The Supremes as well as the tougher-voiced Martha Reeves and the Vandellas. Other record labels and other towns followed the trend. If Wilson Pickett was the most successful of the early solo performers, then Otis Redding became the most charismatic, his death—in an aeroplane crash in 1968 —only clinching the legend. Some singers came almost directly from church to recording studio, like the three daughters, Carolyn, Erma and Aretha, of the Rev. C. L. Franklin, preacher at Detroit's New Bethel Baptist Church, whose sermons were big-sellers on LPs. Aretha Franklin was inspired to sing by hearing Clara Ward, a veteran of the gospel circuit, and her improbable range and ability to project raw feeling ('I like to sound deep and greasy') set her apart from the other girl singers.

But if 'soul' became an international taste, its strength still lay in the black communities, where blues were being rejected in favour of more activist music. Blues were always an outlet for individual emotions, a way of coming to terms with life, but gospel was a traditional vehicle for protest. When the slaves had gathered to sing spirituals they used Biblical events rather like a code, so that the plight of the Israelites and the vision of Canaan took on a much more local significance. It seems entirely logical that not a bar of blues gets played during performances by James Brown, the ghettoes' favourite son, a black man who is successful at the most all-American level. A multi-millionaire, Brown is the owner of three radio stations, a chain of restaurants and an aeroplane called 'The Sex Machine'. His message, expressed not so much in words as in dancing and by his own achievements, is that tomorrow may be better. Brown's slogan, 'Shout it out loud, I'm black and I'm proud', sums up the general situation.

Yet all this would have nothing but sociological importance if James Brown was not a phenomenal performer. Just over forty, shortish and a bit stocky, certainly no more than average as a singer, his authority lies in the way he moves, able to turn the smallest gesture, even dusting off a trouser leg, into a balletic triumph. As artificial as opera, its virtuosity as self-contained as Art Tatum's piano-playing, 'The James Brown Show' is closer to African ritual than to Western art, full of little touches that initiates greet with delight. (When Brown falls to the floor once, twice, thrice, each time having a cloak laid across him but shaking it off, insisting on carrying on, the reference, as everybody present knows, is to his near-legendary weak heart.) Moving round the stage, jabbing an accusing finger at his audience, shrieking 'Soul power', 'Clap yo' hands', sometimes just 'Good', repeated again and again, Brown might be Gagool sniffing out malcontents. But the witch doctor, after all, is not far removed from the black preacher, and Africa lurks behind the mannerisms of 'soul' just as it inspires the forms if not the functions of gospel music.

Below *The Stars of Faith*. Right *Aretha Franklin*. Far right *Rev. Gary Davis, blind street-singer of Harlem*.

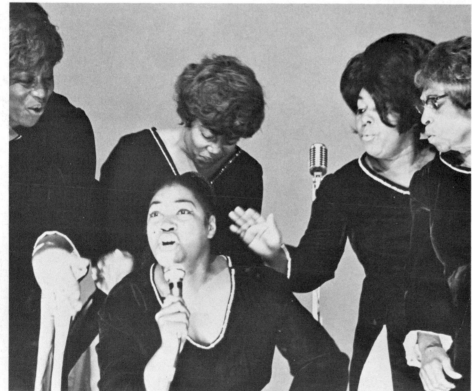

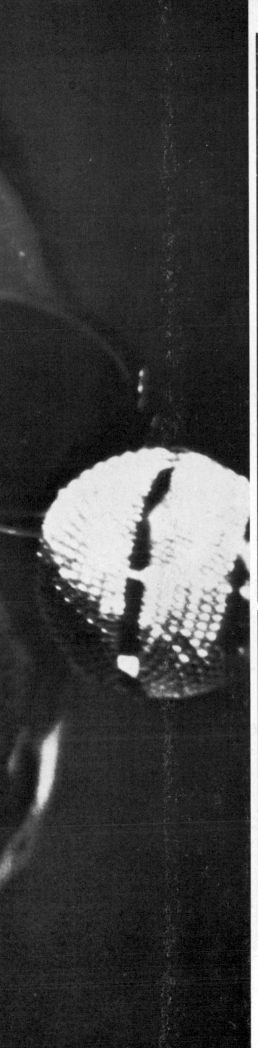

Left *Ray Charles brought the sacred and the secular together.* Top *James Brown.*

Above *The Blind Boys of Mississippi.*

49

# Festival Jazz

Nobody can be absolutely certain when and where the very first jazz festival took place. (What, after all, were some of those long-ago happenings in New Orleans or aboard Mississippi riverboats?) But Randall's Island, near the meeting place of the Harlem and East Rivers, wedged in between the Bronx, Manhattan and Long Island, must be a strong contender for that distinction. An estimated 24,000 people trekked there on 29 May 1938 to hear twenty-four bands perform in a 'Carnival of Swing', put on as a benefit for the local American Federation of Musicians. Those were days when the brasher newspapermen were always stumbling across clarinettists blowing liquorice-sticks, trombonists grappling with slush-pumps, bassists slapping away at dog-houses. Even the reviewer of the New York Times felt obliged to dwell on jitterbugs and alligators who cavorted as Betty Hutton, the singer with the Vincent Lopez Orchestra, bulldozed her way through *Who Stole the Jam?* But the music was better and more righteous than this implies. The little bands of Joe Marsala and Bobby Hackett were both on hand. So was the Duke Ellington Orchestra, reducing the opposition to rubble with one of Ellington's lengthier compositions, *Diminuendo and Crescendo in Blue.* (History repeated itself at Newport eighteen years later, when the Ellington band brought another festival audience to its feet by playing exactly the same piece—but this time with Paul Gonsalves's tenor saxophone providing a marathon interlude between the two parts.)

That affair on Randall's Island, however, lasted for only five-and-three-quarter hours, whereas most people think of a jazz festival as stretching into a second or even a third day. Perhaps it was not surprising that the first festival of this kind should take place in France—within three years of the Second World War ending—because at that time jazz still enjoyed greater prestige in European cultural circles than it did in its homeland. Master-minded by the French critic, Hugues Panassié, the 'first International Jazz Festival' was held alongside the Mediterranean, at Nice in the summer of 1948; it presented a week of concerts by artists who included Mezz

Mezzrow, Rex Stewart, Lucky Thompson and Louis Armstrong's newly-formed Hot Five (with Jack Teagarden, Earl Hines and Sid Catlett). A year later, this time with Panassié's great rival, Charles Delaunay, in charge, a festival in Paris offered a slightly wider range: Sidney Bechet was balanced by Charlie Parker, Miles Davis was there as well as Hot Lips Page. Not to be outdone, Panassié put on a fringe festival at which Leadbelly sang chain-gang songs in the shadow of the Sorbonne, keeping a handkerchief over his left hand to stop young guitarists from copying his fingering.

Not until 1954 did the American jazz festival really come into being. That was the year Elaine and Louis Lorrilard raised the money for a festival

on the grass courts of the nineteenth-century, gabled Casino—the birthplace of American lawn tennis—at Newport, Rhode Island. At five past nine on the Saturday evening, Stan Kenton introduced Eddie Condon ('The Sir Thomas Beecham of jazz'), whose band promptly got to grips with *Muskrat Ramble.* Ella Fitzgerald, Dizzy Gillespie, Lee Konitz and Gerry Mulligan also went on-stand that night, while the producer was George Wein, who has gone on doing the same job every year since then.

Apart from forays into blues, folk

and pop, the pattern has, for better or for worse, stayed roughly the same, with esoteric and avant-garde groups confined to the more thinly attended afternoon sessions, and the big names—even a few out-and-out show-biz people like Frank Sinatra—used to pull in the Saturday and Sunday night audiences. There have been setbacks: a riot in 1960, a near-riot in 1969, the year rock bands were added to the attractions, and—worst of all—a teenage invasion in 1971 which put the Festival's future in peril. Only in 1960 did the ructions have a brighter side: that was when Charlie Mingus organized a splinter festival only a short distance away, featuring Max Roach, Roy Eldridge and a handful of other dissidents.

Four years after the 1954 opening, Monterey, on the opposite coast of the United States, held its first festival, with John Lewis as artistic director. Since then jazz festivals have been put on in Tulsa and New Orleans, in Chicago and at Great South Bay, in Pittsburgh and French Lick, everywhere, in fact, that the music seemed capable of pulling in a crowd and showing a profit. Only Harlem thought of reversing the idea, forgetting about money and taking the festival to the people, performing by sidewalks and in city squares rather than inside giant auditoriums or ball-parks. It was during the summer of 1965 that the Harlem Cultural Council dreamed up the notion of the Jazzmobile, a large bandstand mounted on a truck-bed and towed through the streets with a cargo of famous jazzmen aboard, ending up with a one-hour concert in some part of the borough. Originally intended as publicity for a full-scale festival of the arts, it caught on as a good idea in its own right. By 1968 the 'Friends of Jazzmobile' had persuaded Coca-Cola and the Chemical Bank New York Trust to sponsor the event and bystanders in Brooklyn, Queens and the Bronx, as well as Harlem, were being regaled by musicians and groups ranging from Dizzy Gillespie to Herbie Mann, from Puco and the Latin Soul Brothers to the entire Count Basie orchestra.

Jazz entered a Stately Home in the 1950s, when Lord Montagu staged a series of festivals at Beaulieu Abbey

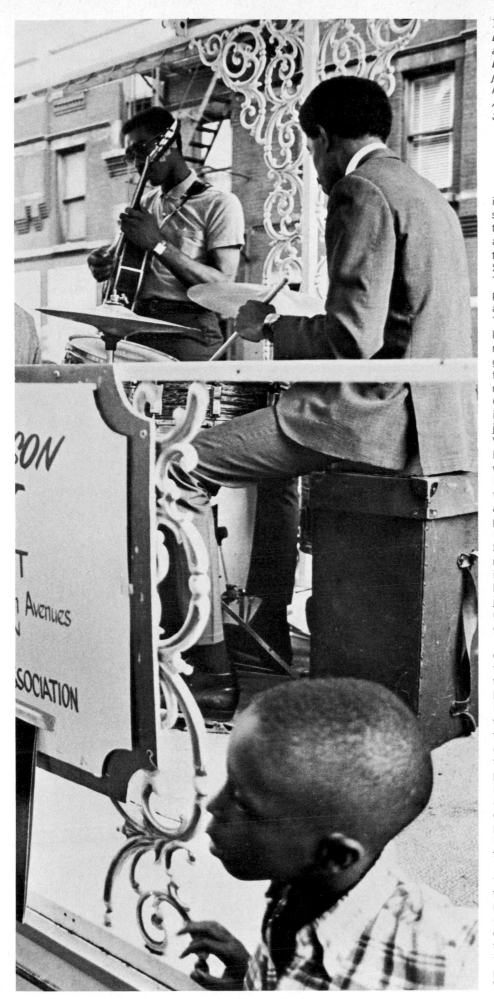

in Hampshire, the music occasionally setting off sympathetic vibrations in the bodywork of a Vauxhall 30/98, a DMS Delage or a bullnose Morris in the Montagu Motor Museum nearby. Since then Britain has had the outdoor 'Jazz and Blues Festival' (blues, even pop, have now almost nudged jazz out) and—up to 1970, anyway—the indoor 'Jazz Expo', a mixture of blues, gospel, lots of mainstream and middlebrow modern, and just a pinch of avant-garde. But the festival concept flourishes more vigorously on the non-English-speaking side of the Channel. Indeed, the map of Europe is dotted with festival centres: not just obvious ones like Frankfurt, Vienna, Berlin (audiences there boo more indiscriminately than anywhere else), Juan-les-Pins or Montreux, but taking in such spots as the island of Yvoir in Belgium, and—again in Belgium—Amourgies, where a pop-and-jazz festival mounted by a French record company had Archie Shepp starting his set at 7.30 in the morning. And there are the goings-on in Prague and Warsaw and elsewhere behind the Iron Curtain, places where jazz organizations are quite likely to end up with a central office block and a grant from the Ministry of Culture.

There are snags, of course. Some entrepreneurs seem more concerned with selling hot dogs and Coca Colas than with presenting good music; bands often get pushed on and off like lots at an auction sale; there are, too, those vast amphitheatres with the sound coming from every direction except the right one. But at its best the festival has a role to play in present-day jazz. Ideally, of course, it should do more than present an array of musicians; works ought to be commissioned from jazz composers, programmes should be given an historical or aesthetic perspective. On the whole European festivals— Montreux is a shining example—seem to be heading in this direction, alive to the fact that jazz is more casual, more inclined to be right (or wrong) on the night than traditional Western concert music is, yet also accepting that it deserves to be presented with the same kind of care which goes into putting on Mozart at Salzburg or Wagner at Bayreuth.

51

# On the Fringe

Jazz musicians, like all embattled artists, view the men on the fringe—promoters, record producers, broadcasters, writers—with mixed feelings. Everyone is glad of a gig or a record date, yet these can lead to squabbling about wages and royalties. Similarly, publicity is always useful but it takes a well-adjusted jazzman to welcome the candour of a bad review. Jazz players, especially black ones, have an artist's responsibility without his status. Some are inclined to be touchy. Others have been pushed around for so long that they are suspicious of the smiler with the contract—or the open notebook. But word soon travels and anyone trying to be honest usually gets the credit for it.

The first man who set out deliberately to record jazz, as distinct from working for a major record label, was a philanthropist anyway. John Hammond, scion of a wealthy New York family, left Yale at weekends to roam the clubs and ginmills of Harlem. In 1932 he learnt record producing the hard way, making three classic sides with Fletcher Henderson's band in just under an hour. (The session had been fixed to begin at 10 a.m. but it was half-past twelve before the last man —bassist John Kirby—rolled up.) Hammond 'discovered' Billie Holiday, Charlie Christian and Count Basie's orchestra, persuaded his brother-in-law, Benny Goodman, to start a band in 1935, and three years later brought blues players up from the South for the 'Spirituals to Swing' concerts at Carnegie Hall. Even today he remains a talent-spotter, signing up the singer and folk-poet, Bob Dylan.

Norman Granz was a film-editor in Hollywood when, in 1944, he began staging informal jazz concerts. Those one-off events ballooned into 'Jazz At The Philharmonic', virtually a travelling jam session, putting players of different styles and periods together and seeing what happened. The jazz could get too boisterous for some critics' taste, yet as well as selling excitement JATP took musicians like Lester Young and Charlie Parker all over the United States and Granz helped a lot of mainstream jazzmen to earn a good living at a time when their music was sadly out of fashion.

No other fringe men have had quite the impact of Hammond and Granz. Nevertheless, the festivals directed by George Wein (at Newport) and Joachim Berendt (in Berlin) are important. And there are other record producers who do more than just twiddle knobs. Teo Macero, once a tenor saxophonist and twelve-tone composer, has been supervising Miles Davis—not the easiest man to order about—since Davis changed labels in 1956. In Britain Denis Preston has always been willing to back his taste, recording artists like Stan Tracey and Indo-Jazz Fusions, while David Howells and Peter Eden have begun sponsoring further-out British jazz.

Television rarely gives jazz a chance, but there have been documentaries— 'Louis Armstrong', 'The Three Faces of Jazz'—of Geoffrey Haydon, and the long series of programmes made by another BBC producer, Terry Henebery, taking in almost everyone from Willie 'The Lion' Smith to Cecil Taylor. On the whole radio is friendlier. Undoubtedly the most famous voice—deep, slow, determined to beat the static—belongs to Willis Conover, reaching thousands on both sides of the Iron Curtain with his US Information Service programme, 'Voice of America'. Billy Taylor, well-known as a pianist and composer, acts as disc jockey for New York's WLIB-FM, a station which puts out a lot of jazz. In Britain the best jazz broadcaster is another musician, Humphrey Lyttelton, opinionated, casual, wittier than most comedians. Plenty of jazz gets played over Continental radio stations, a regular broadcaster from Cologne being Dr Dietrich Schulz-Koehn, who in 1945 demonstrated the priorities of the rabid jazz fan, when, as an officer of the surrendering German garrison at Calais, he began by asking the party of American officers if they had any new Benny Goodman records.

The most important pre-war jazz critic was a Frenchman, Hugues Panassié, author of Hot Jazz, published in Paris in 1934. Not everyone, however, went along with his later view that jazz—'real jazz', as he put it—stopped when the beboppers took over. Gunther Schuller, who once played the French horn with Miles Davis and is currently President of the New England Conservatory of Music, has produced the best musicological analyses of jazz, while the most extensive blues researching has been done by Paul Oliver, a British lecturer in art and architecture. Plenty of sound criticism has been published by the Americans Nat Hentoff, Martin Williams, Leroi Jones (one of the few black writers to have been active on the scene), Ira Gitler and the late Marshall Stearns, by the British writers Max Jones, Stanley Dance, Miles Kington, Ronald Atkins, Alun Morgan, Brian Priestley and Max Harrison, while in France the composer André Hodeir has been a useful antidote to Panassié's fundamentalism. Whitney Balliett of the New Yorker is easily the finest prose writer, able to make a drum solo ricochet off the printed page.

Discography, the listing of personnels, dates, matrix and record numbers, even the particular musicians who take solos, is a branch of scholarship peculiar to jazz. Once again, a Frenchman, Charles Delaunay, did the pioneering. Albert McCarthy (he also edits the British jazz and blues magazine, Jazz Monthly) embarked on Jazz Directory, reaching the letter L—Fred Longshaw, to be exact—before giving up. Jorgen Grunnet Jepsen, a Dane, took over everything from 1942 onward, while another Briton, Brian Rust, friend of the late Nick LaRocca and chief rooter for the Original Dixieland Jazz Band, burrowed back to 1897. Other reference books have been Leonard Feather's Encyclopaedias of Jazz, and —a work of rare diligence—John Chilton's Who's Who Of Jazz, letting in nobody born after 1919 but detailing the saga of Jack Purvis, aviator, mercenary, carpenter, chef, and sometime proprietor of the Miami School of Greek Dancing as well as trumpeter, who drove a baby Austin with a trailer full of cookery books and orchestral scores and ended up leading the prison band at El Paso, Texas.

Far left *Promoter-pianist George Wein.* Top *Record producer Teo Macero.* Bottom *John Hammond.*

# Session Jazz

'Bread is your only friend,' Charlie Parker used to say, meaning not the sliceable sort but the hipster's synonym for money. Parker's admonition also implied that while art may purge the soul it cannot always take care of the bills. For jazz, just like any other art form, is a hazardous profession, menaced by slump, by the faltering imagination, even by the tilting of fashion. No wonder those musicians with the right temperaments and techniques—and Parker, as well as being the wrong colour, had neither—happily cash in on their craftsmanship, helping to tape TV jingles, tripping nostalgically down Memory Lane, backing up the newest pop star. But whatever the task, it usually involves visiting a recording studio, one of the global village's essential services, sharing with airports and luxury hotels a spotless anonymity.

It all got going in the 1920s. Men like Red Nichols, Miff Mole, Eddie Lang and Adrian Rollini were perpetually hurrying from one New York studio to another. Collectors of old 78s discover them taking solos in the unlikeliest surroundings. They were all-round pros, able to adjust their playing to most kinds of music, squeezing in a bit of jazz whenever they could. To give an idea of just how busy those sessionmen could be, Benny Goodman, a clarinettist much in demand, played on no fewer than 58 sessions during the first seven months of 1931, making 175 recordings actually issued on discs, including *Mama Inez* by Enrique Madriguera's Havana Casino Orchestra ('with laughing effects') and Ben Selvin's *My Sweet Tooth Says I Wanna (But My Wisdom Tooth Says No)* as well as the Charleston Chasers' classic *Basin Street Blues*. In addition, Goodman worked six nights a week in the pit orchestra for George Gershwin's 'Girl Crazy', played weekend dance dates and did his share of broadcasting and film sound-tracks.

The pace has, if anything, hotted up recently. Bernie Glow sat in the brass sections of the Artie Shaw, Boyd Raeburn and Woody Herman bands before he went free-lance; now he is one of the most sought-after lead trumpet players in New York. Glow normally starts his first session at nine or ten in the morning, then does another from two to five, usually finishing off with an evening session from seven to ten. With the time taken driving between Manhattan and his house in Great Neck, it adds up to a thirteen- or fourteen-hour working day. Many musicians could use the money and have the qualifications (Glow plays flugelhorn and piccolo trumpet as well as ordinary trumpet, while reed players are expected to double on four or five instruments), yet still balk at leading this kind of life. Nevertheless, a surprising number of jazzmen manage to combine staying creative with taking on regular session jobs.

Perhaps the best-known is Clark Terry. Even when he was with the Duke Ellington Orchestra, Terry prided himself on his professionalism, playing his trumpet right-handed one night, left-handed the next, cultivating ambidextrousness in case he ever injured a finger. In addition Terry is one of a small number of black musicians who have broken down the long-standing prejudice against employing any other than white men in the studios. (This situation, even worse in Los Angeles than in New York, improves surely although much too slowly.) Another is Richard Davis, a bassist whose inventiveness is matched by a brilliant technique. In London, the Canadian trumpeter Kenny Wheeler moves unconcernedly from the freest kind of jazz to the unhippest sort of TV show, an improviser of world class as well as one of the best readers and section men in Europe.

But the average jazz musician ventures into a studio much more rarely. Generally it is to record or broadcast his own kind of music, a trickier business than simply performing at a club. 'Like I stand up, and like I blow, and like people say "Crazy!",' was the answer a famous American saxophonist gave to a Continental jazz critic pestering him to outline his aesthetic philosophy. Yet even that extrovert has to make concessions in a recording studio. Not only must he avoid knocking a microphone with the bell of his instrument but no audience is there to enthuse and encourage. Even worse,

Above *Dave Holland (bass), Jack De Johnette (drums), Miles Davis (trumpet) being recorded for TV and disc during a concert in Berlin.* Right *Jimmy Hopps in the studio.* Far right *Jazz session-men Bob Brookmeyer (trombone), Clark Terry (flugelhorn).*

drummers get boxed away from bass players, entire rhythm sections are separated from front-lines, empathy is sacrificed for the sake of a clean balance. The only known bit of film showing Charlie Parker has him miming to a solo he had already recorded—for the sake of better sound quality. It is somehow symbolic that he smirks unashamedly at the camera. Or perhaps he was smiling, like a man catching sight of his very best friend.

# Jazz & Pop

Squinting down the nose at pop music is a habit jazzmen cultivated fairly late in the day, once they had become status-conscious. After all, Bix Beiderbecke was positively cock-a-hoop at joining Paul Whiteman's orchestra (the $300-a-week he got may have helped, a small fortune in 1927), while the best New Orleans bands played *Yaaka Hula Hickey Dula* and other First World War song-hits as well as rags and stomps and blues. Ever since jazz surfaced, in fact, it has cohabited with other sorts of American popular music, actually sharing its Afro-American background with such modern dance steps as the Charleston, the Twist, even the sedate-seeming Fox Trot. Quite a few famous jazzmen have doubled as song-writers, from Duke Ellington—*In A Sentimental Mood, Solitude, I Let A Song Go Out Of My Heart* and dozens of others—to Fats Waller, whose *Ain't Misbehavin'* could be mistaken for a Louis Armstrong solo. (The verse of Hoagy Carmichael's *Star Dust* is another instance of a song-writer echoing a jazz soloist, in this case Bix.) Waller also squandered his piano playing and satirical banter on some of the sorriest Tin Pan Alley numbers of the 1930s, just as Coleman Hawkins picked one of the best, Johnny Green's *Body and Soul*, as the skeleton for a masterpiece. Benny Goodman would never have become 'King Of Swing' had his band not played tunes that young white Americans could identify with, while even bebop lived off the backs—well, the chords—of the best Broadway composers. In their turn, pop music arrangers borrowed jazz devices—Duke Ellington's exoticism, Count Basie's riffs, even Charlie Parker's quirky harmonic stance—but carefully watered them down. And nowadays half the discs which nose their way into the Top Twenty seem to be built around the twelve-bar blues.

Yet jazz musicians were traditionally reluctant to work in commercial bands (Bix's elation was exceptional, even premature), looking on such a job as a chore done solely to lay hands on some ready cash. But today plenty of good young musicians play in rock bands from choice as often as necessity. The main reason is the change which

has taken place in pop ever since, sometime during the 1950s, it stopped being a matter of hit-songs and based itself on groups. At its boldest, as rock or progressive rock, pop music, just like jazz, is a craft—occasionally even an art—of performance, actually sharing with jazz common roots in blues and gospel. Where jazz flashed through the entire cycle of European concert music—folk, classical, romantic, neo-classical, neo-romantic—in about sixty years, pop looks like doing it inside twenty. And the same kind of aesthetic compulsions have been at work, the more ambitious musicians quickly growing discontented with providing a background to dancing or drinking.

*Gary Burton: bending notes, mixing genres. Left Larry Coryell, jazz guitarist with a fuzz-box.*

Yet as well as similarities there are also differences. Most obvious is the relative rigidity of the rock beat—eight to a bar instead of the traditional, more flexible, four beats of jazz. Another is how guitars are used; not just the amplification—after all, Charlie Christian started the whole thing off in the 1930s—but the physical dimension of a pop guitarist's playing, the way it demands to be seen as much as heard, relying on sound more than line, embellishing rather than improvising, exploiting sensation as jazz very seldom does.

For a long while this electronic ambience marked the point where jazz

ended and pop began, yet bit by bit jazz players have been plugging in as well. The quartet led by Gary Burton, a virtuoso of the vibraphone, able to bend notes in a way nobody else can, included Larry Coryell, one of the first guitarists to straddle the two idioms, using fuzz-box techniques as well as straight jazz methods. (Both Burton and Coryell spent a lot of time working—and listening—in Nashville, which explains why, unlike most jazz-rock groups, the Burton Quartet has a distinct country-and-western side to it.) Steve Swallow, Burton's bass player, alternated between using string bass and bass guitar, an instrument central to the strategy of jazz-rock. Louder than the string-bass, its patterns often taking on the status of a theme, the bass guitar focusses the improvising of a group like Nucleus, led by the British trumpeter Ian Carr.

Similarly, Nucleus's drummer, John Marshall, deploys the eight-to-a bar rhythms of pop, yet, just like Jon Hiseman, another excellent technician who led Colosseum, he cannot conceal his jazz origins, any more than Colosseum's saxophonist, Dick Heckstall-Smith, could smother his allegiance to Sidney Bechet, Wardell Gray and John Coltrane. (Not that drummers have to come up inside jazz to be good, a fact made plain by Keith Moon's drumming with The Who, a pop group owing nothing to either concert music or jazz.) Perhaps the commonest fault is an uneasy electicism, the way organists slip in quotes from Bach chorales, the way singers get included for conformist reasons rather than because they fit the music. At times Colosseum showed symptoms of this; so did Manfred Mann's Chapter Three, an adventurous group led by a South African pianist who scuffled for work in London before moving into pop.

Because jazz musicians are traditionally suspicious of singers, the majority of jazz-rock groups (as distinct from rock-jazz ones) manage with a minimum of vocalizing. Yet a surprising number of jazz composers—Eddie Gale, Michael Garrick, Andrew Hill, Bobby Hutcherson and Mike Westbrook among them—have begun using voices as part of the orchestral fabric. Nobody,

however, shows signs of exploring the kind of send-ups pioneered by Frank Zappa, anti-hero and arch-debunker, sometime leader of the Mothers of Invention, a guitarist who has jammed with Archie Shepp and composed a set of pieces for the violinist, Jean-Luc Ponty. Zappa's virtue is his unexpectedness, working like shock-therapy, deflating not only the obviously banal—Hollywood mores, the America of apple-pie and Mother's Day—but would-be liberators as well ('This year's Flower Power is fighting in the streets'). The same sort of all-roundness, yet lacking Zappa's savage eye, is found in two other American groups, Chicago and Blood, Sweat and Tears. Most of their players sport musical degrees and dabble in jazz rather as they dabble in pop ('We listen to everyone from Bach and Stravinsky to Varese,' says Robert Lamm, organist with Chicago). Clever, often witty (the adaptations of Eric Satie's *Trois Gymnopédies* on Blood, Sweat and Tears' first LP was exactly in character), they all too frequently proffer jazz solos stuffed with commonplaces of the 1950s. (Earlier on, however, BS&T included the trumpeter Randy Brecker, very lyrical, very inventive, who later worked with Horace Silver.) Easily the most creative of the rock-jazz groups

has been Flock, complete with a violinist, Jerry Goodman, who once played with the Chicago Civic Symphony Orchestra ('They were so uptight with me, they didn't like my hair'), but has concocted his own eclectic yet dazzling style, at one moment see-sawing like a country fiddler, at the next taking the blues apart.

Only 17 when he became Miles Davis's drummer, Tony Williams helped to realign the *raison d'être* of Davis's Sextet, turning, in the process, into the most miraculous user of pop rhythms. In 1969 he joined forces with Larry Young, the jazz organist, and two British musicians, bass guitarist Jack Bruce and guitarist John McLaughlin. Calling themselves Lifetime, they launched into exhaustive and exhausting improvisations, dense, complex, loud ('It's the primitiveness of rock that appeals to me, not the rhythms,' says Williams. 'I like the basic body sounds, not the rock "feel" but the energy'). By comparison, Soft Machine, an all-British group—the name comes from a novel by William Burroughs—seemed positively formal, even abstract, especially in compositions by its organist, Mike Ratledge. Some impinged on the microscopic world of Terry Riley, the 'straight' avant-garde

composer, short phrases interlocking like pieces in a jigsaw puzzle, constant repetition magnifying tiny differences. But the group's free-wheeling side came through in pieces devised by Hugh Hopper, the bass guitarist, and Robert Wyatt, a drummer who often ended up playing stripped to the waist. (The saxophonist, Elton Dean, started out in an Irish show band and commutes between Soft Machine and Keith Tippett's jazz group.) Most of these musicians began by listening to Cecil Taylor, Ornette Coleman and John Coltrane, even if sometimes they make a point of emphasizing their apartness from present-day jazz. ('Jazz drumming taught me what not to do,' Robert Wyatt once declared. 'For me, it's really all down to James Brown's rhythm section.') Its image and sound in tune with the freakier sort of pop group, yet improvising with a logic any jazz fan ought to recognize, the Soft Machine has embodied a significant and satisfying overlap. Maybe it even hints at what lies ahead in the 1980s.

Above *Trumpeter Randy Brecker, once with Blood, Sweat and Tears.*
Right *Frank Zappa, guitarist, composer, arch debunker, sometime leader of the Mothers of Invention.*

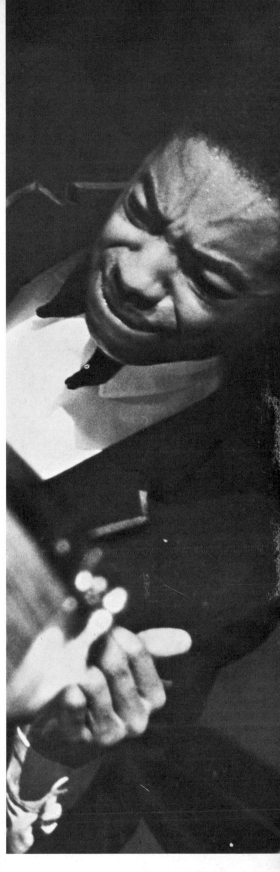

*Two drummer-leaders: Above* Tony Williams (Lifetime), *left* Jon Hiseman (Colosseum). *Far left* Pop-blues *guitarist Jimi Hendrix.*

61

# Blues

Blues mean different things to different people: a set of harmonies, a climate of feeling, even, for smart white dancers in the 1920s, a snail's-pace tempo. The word already had an undertone of melancholy by Elizabethan times ('having the blues' is no modern malaise) but not until the end of the nineteenth century did blues as we know them—generally twelve bars long, with a three-line stanza—come into being, probably evolving out of field-hollers, sung by men working alone or with just a mule. For a time blues remained self-contained, the singer usually accompanying himself on his guitar, even after the most expert performers—Charlie Patton, Blind Lemon Jefferson, Rambling Thomas, these are among the earliest we know about—started using their talents to earn a living, often spending half their lives trudging from one Southern town to another. Blues lyrics dealt with basic human needs and anxieties: the two-timing woman, the jinx that brings bad luck, a whole landscape of innocent hope and evil ways. Sunset or morning star, bedbug or bollweevil, Northbound rattler or Cadillac car—the blues singer took his images from the world he moved in.

Purely instrumental blues belonged to the next phase, starting with New Orleans bands playing blues tunes that had a melodic identity. Bit by bit the chord sequence became a ground-plan, allowing soloists to improvise for as long or as little as they chose. Half the jazz repertoire, possibly half the classic jazz records, spring from that stubborn group of harmonies, infinitely variable, infinitely expressive. And just as the meditative blues of country singers co-existed with the so-called 'classic blues'—more knowing, more dramatic, much more rhetorical—of women such as Bessie Smith and Ma Rainey, so a whole species of jazz bands featured blues in various guises. (Not until the arrival of bebop, with its harmonic and rhythmic complications, did rhythm-and-blues bands hive off and exist apart from jazz.) During the 1920s and early 1930s, the southwest, a huge territory taking in Texas, Arkansas, Missouri, Kansas and Oklahoma, was patrolled by Walter Page's Blue Devils, Troy Floyd's Shadowland Orchestra and scores of other itinerant bands, performing before audiences which demanded plenty of blues. Boogie-woogie pianists worked the southwest too, playing in mining towns and railroad construction camps as well as prosperous centres like St Louis and Kansas City. (At one time the style was called 'Fast Western' because it was mostly heard on the western side of the Mississippi river.)

Between the wars only Chicago rivalled Kansas City for civic squalor. Thomas J. Pendergast, the most powerful city boss of his generation, ruled there from 1927 until his death in 1938. But low-life arts have a habit of flourishing where liquor laws are winked at and gambling gets encouraged. It was true of jazz and blues. Kansas City even sired a new breed of stand-up singers, their manner half-legato, half-recitative, epitomised by Joe Turner, a massive bar-tender, whose voice ('You didn't have micro-phones or nothing in those days') soared above the chatter at Piney Brown's Sunset Crystal Palace, boasting of his virility ('Going to eagle rock you mama 'till your face turns cherry red') or analyzing the human dilemma ('You're so beautiful but you got to die some day'). At the badly ventilated Reno Club, Count Basie put together the orchestra he was to conquer New York with, while a few years later the best local band, Jay McShann's, had Charlie Parker sitting in its saxophone section. Elsewhere in the southwest, in Oklahoma City, Charlie Christian found out how to make the best use of the new amplified guitar. T-Bone Walker, from Texas, built upon Christian's jazz style in adapting the instrument for blues, realizing, just like Christian, that it could now hold its own with saxophones and trumpets. Walker's flamboyant playing went with his taste in showmanship (he often took a chorus one-handed or with the guitar behind his back, sometimes even lying full-length on the floor) and was later taken over by B. B. King, once a Mississippi plantation worker, who

*Blues pianist and singer Roosevelt Sykes relaxing with British Rail.*

added traditional bottle-neck techniques but using finger vibrato at high volume instead of actually sliding a bottle-neck or steel along the strings. The result was a glittering yet economical style of his own, which in its turn rubbed off on young guitarists like Otis Rush, Freddy King and Buddy Guy, all adept at contrasting long whining notes with breakneck runs.

The fresh, sometimes startling timbres which crept into blues were really the sounds of the city, reflecting both a faster pace of living and a more threatening ambience. One after another, country singers who caught the train to Chicago found the city entering into their music as well as their souls. It had happened to Sonny Boy Williamson from Tennessee, to Jazz Gillum from Mississippi, to Washboard Sam (his real name was Robert Brown) from Arkansas, and to dozens of others during the 1920s and 1930s; it happened again to a post-war generation. The kind of transformation which took place, familiar yet decisive, can be glimpsed in the way country blues formed the basis of the Chicago blues that flourished in the 1950s, a development revolving round Muddy Waters's little band. Muddy Waters (actually McKinley Morganfield) was born in Rolling Fork but raised in Clarksdale, Mississippi. He started by playing acoustic guitar and harmonica in a local string band, and the same instrumentation, but sharpened up, heavily amplified, flanked him at Smitty's Corner on 35th and Indiana streets, where, harsh-voiced, proud as a stallion, he roused women into flinging purses and house-keys at his feet whenever he sang *I've Got My Mojo Working* or *I'm A Man*. Yet although blues like these were all the rage on Chicago's South Side, in other parts of the United States they were scarcely heard by black record-buyers, let alone white ones.

When blues eventually arrived in the Top Twenty it was as rock 'n' roll, mixed with country-and-western jauntiness. Bill Haley's Comets obviously owed more to Nashville than to Chicago or Indianapolis, but Elvis Presley was different—at first, anyway. As a teenager in Memphis he heard blues singers on radio and discs. One of his earliest hits, *That's All Right*, had previously been recorded by Arthur 'Big Boy' Crudup, while *Hound Dog* was only a moderate success for Big Mama Thornton before Presley took the song over. For a moment it looked as if a genuinely grown-up idiom, one that faced the facts of life, was about to disrupt the cardboard world of American popular music. But the lyrics soon got bowdlerized, the major record companies rushed out 'cover copies' by their white stars of likely hits by black singers, rock 'n' roll got turned into rock and roll, prepackaged, about

as inspirational as sliced bread. Yet the blues were to make a comeback, but this time from an entirely unexpected quarter, travelling across the Atlantic.

Europeans had always doted upon blues singers and players. By the 1950s a steady stream of bluesmen was flowing out of America, heading for London, most of them country singers because European tastes favoured familiar styles rather than new-fangled ones. So Big Bill Broonzy, the first off the mark, quickly switched to the folk-blues he had half-forgotten instead of playing the small-band blues he was known for in Chicago. After him came Sonny Terry and Brownie McGhee, Speckled Red, Muddy Waters (British blues fans got upset when he plugged in his electric guitar), Roosevelt Sykes, Little Brother Montgomery and many others, including singers who had fallen into obscurity, even been thought to have died— Sleepy John Estes, Son House, Skip James, Bukka White, Big Joe Williams— as well as some, like John Lee Hooker, Lightnin' Hopkins and Howlin' Wolf, who had only just been discovered or rediscovered. A prime mover in bringing blues artists to Europe was the trombonist and bandleader Chris Barber, always a keen *aficionado*. And other British blues fanatics were about to move from hero-worshipping old-timers to learning the craft themselves.

St Patrick's Night, 1962, not only saw plenty of Irishmen sporting shamrocks and downing treble whiskies, it also witnessed the opening—in Ealing, once the home of British film comedies—of London's first rhythm-and-blues club. On the stand was Blues Incorporated, led by Alexis Korner, half-Greek, half-Austrian, something of a veteran blues guitarist and scholar. Alongside him stood Cyril Davies, a panel-beater by trade, playing harmonica but even better when handling the bulky 12-string guitar. An extraordinary assortment of talent filtered in and out of Korner's various bands during the next few years, from Mick Jagger (the Rolling Stones originally got together to deputize for Blues Incorporated when a broadcast clashed with a regular gig) to Jack Bruce and Ginger Baker. Other jazz musicians—Dick Heckstall-Smith, Graham Bond, Ray Warleigh, Art Themen—helped to create a band-style which hovered somewhere between Muddy Waters and Charlie Mingus. It was the beginning of the British r-and-b boom, which, aided by the Beatles up in Liverpool, would introduce white American audiences to a music that had started out in the ghettoes of Chicago and Detroit.

Ironies abound in every human situation. At almost the exact moment that white American and British youngsters began accepting blues, the black American society started rejecting

them. What young blacks went for was gospel-based 'soul', enshrining a very different set of social values. Blues had been a music of acceptance, purgative but consolatory, a necessary art for a people who could do little but endure. Black activists now thought those attitudes reactionary, black teenagers found the style old-fashioned. In Chicago the middle-aged bluesmen sang in bars that were half-empty; they had, in any case, contributed to the decline by down-grading the lyrics, turning blues more and more into just a background for dancing or drinking, music that could every bit as easily be supplanted by another sort. Yet blues remained vital to jazz, an emotional stimulus for even the furthest-out players. And dedicated blues performers continued to emerge, even if they worked outside the black community. (Jimi Hendrix, American-born, the most original of the young guitarists, had to go to Britain to make his name.) It looks as if a long tradition has suddenly skipped a generation, for although blues go on being sung and played they no longer seem essential to that society which up to now has always nurtured, inspired and needed them.

Below *T-Bone Walker*. Right *Mississippi singer Big Joe Williams*.

64

Big Mama Thornton,
originator of Hound Dog.
Below *Country bluesmen:
Hammie Nixon (harmonica),
Sleepy John Estes (guitar).
Left* B. B. King.

Four guitar-playing bluesmen.
Below *Albert King*. Bottom *Dr. Isaiah Ross (also playing harmonica in a harness)*. Left *Chicago blues king Muddy Waters — originally McKinley Morganfield from Clarksdale, Mississippi.* Far left *Buddy Guy*.

# The Singers

One of the big differences between jazz and conventional European music is the way the jazz player's sound resembles the human voice, reflecting its shifts and shades of meaning. This happens whenever Cootie Williams pushes a plunger-mute into his trumpet, Ben Webster's tenor saxophone blows a shuddering cadenza, or, just to show that things still are what they used to be, Ornette Coleman conjures his alto saxophone to lament or to rejoice. Musicologists call it 'vocalized tone', which is another way of saying that jazzmen sing on their horns. It seems odd, therefore, that so much squabbling should have gone on down the years over whether such a creature as a jazz singer exists.

Musicians themselves often resented singers interrupting the jazz, looking on them as so many sops to commercialism. Some were, others were not: Bessie Smith, for example, a blues singer but one who always worked with jazzmen. A decade later, in the 1930s, Billie Holiday turned songs to her own ends, trimming the melodies and simplifying the harmonies as ruthlessly as any trumpeter or saxophonist. Even more remarkably, she caused the words to come alive in a way the lyric-writers could never have hoped for. When Bessie Smith sang the poetry was already there, inside the blues, but Billie Holiday arrived when blues were in retreat; the songs she had to tackle were trilled in Broadway shows and crooned at the movies. Her achievement was to create the poetry with her voice, translating the sentimental into the emotional.

Billie Holiday had already made her first record, with a Benny Goodman pick-up group, by the time that Ella Fitzgerald, singing *Lost In A Fog* with a pianist who muffed the chords, got booed off-stage during amateur night at Harlem's Lafayette Theatre. But from then on Ella never put a foot wrong. She joined Chick Webb's band at the Savoy Ballroom—Webb made her stick to up-tempo numbers for the whole of the first year—and when the hunch-backed drummer died she launched upon the solo career that has taken in Song Books and Beatles numbers as well as countless scatted choruses of *Lady Be Good*. Next in

line was Sarah Vaughan, coeval with the beboppers, weaving her way through the tricky new chord changes with a sultry arrogance, technically the most extraordinary singer ever to turn up in jazz.

Left *Sheila Jordan.* Below *Salena Jones shares her birthplace – Newport News, Virginia – with Ella Fitzgerald and Pearl Bailey.*

Men sang too, even if, to begin with, they were mostly musicians helping out. Louis Armstrong for one, Jack Teagarden, the earliest instance of glamour in jazz, for another. Arguments have been advanced on behalf of Bing Crosby, especially in his early, swashbuckling days, and Frank Sinatra, but they seemed to occupy the in-between territory—more cut-off in pre-rock days than now—dividing jazz proper from the purlieus of Tin Pan Alley. And words were not always necessary. Armstrong had fallen back on nonsense syllables as early as 1926, Cab Calloway gave the practice a frantic dimension, and by midway through the 1930s Leo Watson, his arm bent, moving in and out like a trombonist's, was improvising gibberish with a mathematician's logic and a sensualist's ecstasy. In Kansas City—and, afterwards, at Greenwich Village's Cafe Society—Big Joe Turner half-sang, half-shouted against Pete Johnson's eight-to-a-bar playing, while Jimmy Rushing's paunch wobbled as he roared *Good Morning Blues* in front of the Basie band. But Turner and Rushing were really blues singers, part of a separate tradition.

Most girl singers of the 1940s and 1950s listened hard to Billie or Ella or Sarah. Some added touches of their own, like Anita O'Day, originally inspired—jazz is full of little ironies—by Martha Raye belting out *Mr Paganini*, then coming up the hard way, singing at dance marathons before she joined Gene Krupa's band in 1941. Seventeen years later, aided by a black-and-white picture-hat, she stole the show in 'Jazz On A Summer's Day', filmed at the 1958 Newport Festival and one of the few feature-length movies to treat jazz on its own terms. Anita O'Day, of course, was white. Pearl Bailey was black and sounded it, using a few too many 'point' numbers for some people to take her seriously as a jazz singer, but incarnating Bessie Smith's growl and truculent sense of humour. Carmen McRae's style was lighter, more svelte, her manner slightly flip and dead-pan, similar to that of Annie Ross, a Scots girl who grew up in America and first attracted notice by fitting hip lyrics to jazz solos. Yet it was Annie Ross's treatments of ballads

that mattered, for she could give words a Brechtian detachment. Brechtian too, but in a different way, was Abbey Lincoln, wife of the drummer Max Roach, mainly because she sang songs of protest, about a black African past, a black American present.

Lambert, Hendricks and Ross could be a firm of wig-makers or a half-back line. In fact they were a trio of singers following up Annie Ross's trick—she was the Ross, of course, doing the high-up trumpet parts—of putting words to jazz instrumentals. Jon Hendricks eventually went out as a solo performer, still indulging in his taste for scatting like a tenor saxophonist. A blues singer who has worked with jazzmen a lot is Jimmy Witherspoon, stretching his phrases across the bar-lines, at his best sounding nearly as sensual as Joe Turner. The blues also left their mark on Mose Allison, a white man from Mississippi, who played stubbly piano and had a voice like a corn-crake.

But after the hub-bub of the Fifties came—in America, at any rate—the silence of the Sixties, for no young black girls seemed to be singing jazz at all. This was caused by the spread of soul music, the rise of Tamla-Motown. Singers who a decade earlier might have been belting out *Just One Of Those Things* in a New York supper club could earn much more money in black pop. Anyone searching for the successor to Bessie Smith would have to seek out Martha Reeves (of Martha and the Vandellas), who took the style a step further than Pearl Bailey, into an area at once newer and older. The oldness lay in the folk roots—gospel even more than the blues—of black pop music. Twenty years earlier Aretha Franklin would have been taking on Billie Holiday. Now she could not properly be called a jazz singer at all. Which is why most of the good new-comers were white, even European.

Cleo Laine, half-West Indian, was born in Southall, an industrial suburb of London. She started by singing with John Dankworth's orchestra, married her bandleader, then branched out artistically, breaking into the Arts

Festival circuit with recitals that mixed Billy Strayhorn songs with settings of Shakespeare, Auden and Eliot, even pieces specially written by the young classical composer, Richard Rodney Bennett. Over in Holland there was Rita Reys, while up in Norway Karin Krog had started expanding the function of the jazz singer, rejecting the traditional reliance upon words, using—rather like the British singer, Norma Winstone—scat-singing in a wider, more free-ranging way. And there is irony in the fact that easily the best singer to work with Duke Ellington's orchestra since Ivie Anderson has been the Swedish soprano, Alice Babs, who performed at Ellington's second Sacred Concert in January 1968.

The newer Americans have mostly been middle-of-the-roaders like Marlena Shaw, who worked with Count Basie, or Nina Simone, develop-ing from nondescript beginnings into a tigerish performer, more menacing than Eartha Kitt, as racially aware as Abbey Lincoln. More obviously unusual is the black male singer Leon Thomas ('Africa is where *I* am'), importing the yodel into jazz, his scatting not all that different from the

festooning found in *Tarana*, the Indian vocal music. But the most satisfying artist, emotionally as well as formally, remained obscure, her quality recognized by only a handful of musicians and jazz writers.

Despite having lived in New York for over twenty years, Sheila Jordan has made only one LP, although she sang a far-out version of Governor Jimmy Davis's tear-jerker, *You Are My Sunshine*, on a George Russell record. British jazz *aficionados* almost broke into cheers when she appeared at Ronnie Scott's Club in London, even if one night she suffered the bizarre accolade of being heckled by the Kray twins. Yet Sheila Jordan still earns most of her living by working as a secretary rather than from music, a curious irony for a performer who transcends her material just as Billie Holiday did, projecting with an intensity which comes from knowing about life as well as art. Nobody, not even the most embittered sideman, would have qualms about calling her a jazz singer.

Below *Ella Fitzgerald*. Above left *Sarah Vaughan*. Right *Cleo Laine, married to composer-bandleader John Dankworth.*

# Big Bands

Like fast bowlers and heavy-weight boxers, big bands promise a whiff of extra excitement, of the headier sort of drama. Yet because these bands' styles were usually tailored by arrangers, the most fashion-conscious operatives in jazz, they tend—all but the best ones, anyway—to stay fixed in a period, typifying instead of transcending. It helps to explain the schism between those who look on the traditional big band—brass, reeds, rhythm, all safe and tidy—as a kind of musical dinosaur, and those—mostly on the untrendy side of forty—for whom the same bands symbolize a vanished Paradise, that era when you could pick out the fellows from the girls, John Wayne rode shot-gun for the good guys and Glenn Miller kept on playing *String of Pearls*.

The spin-down began soon after the boom-years of the 1930s, a period when it seemed as if every sideman was starting up on his own account. The Second World War made it hard to keep a band together, and harder still to replace musicians who got called up. Peace-time brought alterations in social habits. Dance halls which had provided a steady working circuit suddenly seemed to be emptying. By the 1960s, in any case, teenagers were dancing differently, moving to post-Presley rhythms. There was, too, the shift from Hit Parade tunes to Top Twenty discs, the focussing of attention on the singer or the group rather than the song, the fact that, just as in jazz, the performance meant more than what was being performed. Big bands, quicker to feel the pinch than small groups, began folding up.

That Duke Ellington, Count Basie and Woody Herman, even, in a more haphazard way, Stan Kenton, were still doing the rounds at the start of the 1970s is partly because quality generally endures, partly because all of them can rely on support from people who became fans twenty, thirty—in Ellington's case, maybe forty—years ago. And Ellington's songwriting past, taking in *Mood Indigo, Satin Doll, Sophisticated Lady* and dozens of other much-requested numbers, attracts a separate audience, one which does not necessarily grasp just how unique the Ellington ensemble is. Ever since those days, when he led a band at

the Kentucky Club, a basement cafe on 49th and Broadway, before moving to the Cotton Club in December 1927, Ellington has operated in the same way, choosing his musicians carefully. Most of them stay a long, long time. It was in June 1927 that the 17-year-old Harry Carney played his first gig with the band—at Nuttings-on-the-Charles, near Boston—yet Carney's baritone still gives body to Ellington's present-day saxophone section. Similarly, Johnny Hodges, apart from a brief foray into bandleading during the 1950s, never budged from the Ellington ranks between 1928 and his death forty-two years later. Nowadays nobody expects Ellington, just a year older than the century, to go in for the kind of adventuring he did as a young man, yet his orchestra remains one of the outstanding musical phenomena of modern times.

'If you think the saxes are out of tune you should listen to the brass.

And if you think the brass are out of tune, why just listen to the whole band.' That kind of disgruntled reaction was typical of quite a few of the smarter New York musicians who packed into the Famous Door to hear Count Basie's orchestra—stacked in tiers on the tiny bandstand—when it arrived from Kansas City, via Chicago, in the winter of 1936. Yet rough though that original Basie orchestra may have sounded, it brought to big band jazz a tingling excitement, even a sense of urgency, as well as the most relaxed rhythm section in history. There were lots of blues, plenty of riffs and at least one authentic giant among the soloists—Lester Young. Latterly the situation has almost been reversed. Although a born gambler where horses are concerned, Basie has learnt to play it safe musically, teaching the band to swing almost out of habit, opting for precision and for reliable rather than trail-blazing sidemen.

If Duke Ellington's reputation was built upon composing for his own hand picked ensemble, and Count Basie's upon 'head' arrangements— more or less cooked up on the stand—

that allowed a fifteen-piece orchestra to swing like a small group, Woody Herman has specialized in hiring good men and seeing they do what he wants them to. Nobody else is so adept at taking a bunch of raw youngsters and whipping them into a close-knit band. Right at the start, Herman went in for the lighter-tinged kind of blues; halfway through the 1940s his arrangers packaged bebop harmonies and ideas in a big band setting and aimed them at a national audience; a later orchestra was famous for its saxophone section of three tenors (one blown by Stan Getz) and a baritone. Just as an inevitable part of an Ellington concert is the medley of past successes, a Herman programme is likely to include the pre-war *Wood-choppers' Ball* (a British pop group, Ten Years After, gave it yet another lease of life in 1970), the fast twelve-bar blues *Caldonia*, getting speedier and speedier since the band first played it in 1945, and *Four Brothers*, just as Jimmy Giuffre originally scored it for the saxophones. Nowadays Herman woos a younger age-group with pop material arranged in his own style, a practice also followed by Buddy Rich, although Rich's ventures into rock territory—he won cheers from the crowds at Fillmore East—are helped by his obvious virtuosity. The drummer all other drummers hero-worship, a veteran of the Tommy Dorsey and Harry James orchestras, Rich also happens to be a salty ad-libber, his persona hovering somewhere between uptight Sinatra and Bogart as Sam Spade.

But the zeitgeist gets pursued most unrelentingly by the Don Ellis Orchestra. Ellis took the old-style big band as a starting-point, threw in some of Stan Kenton's romanticism, and has added Oriental trimmings (he once worked with the Hindustani Jazz Quartet) and a penchant for recherché time-signatures that even Dave Brubeck must gasp at. ('The only thing Don does in 4/4 is *Take Five*,' Charlie Haden once remarked.) Ellis claims that his big band was the first to play pure rock and roll. A trumpeter who was already deep into the avant-garde by the start of the 1960s, Ellis nowadays performs in a nervously brilliant fashion, sounding like a highbrow Harry James, using a custom-built trumpet with a fourth valve for squeezing out quarter-tones, flanked by echo units and tape loops that allow him to blow duets, trios, even quartets with himself.

But these are all regular bands, working, if their agent is canny enough, week in, week out. Not every musician wants to lead the kind of life that one-night stands involve. For example, during a single month in 1969 the Count Basie Orchestra journeyed from Florida to North Carolina, on to Kansas, Oklahoma, Texas, California

and Arizona, then back to Kansas before doing the rounds of Iowa, Illinois, New York and Connecticut. Many musicians prefer to spend their days in the New York or Los Angeles studios, only playing jazz—more or less for fun—in their spare time. This has spawned a new breed of orchestras, sometimes known as 'rehearsal bands' yet stuffed with professionals and taking on club and concert dates, even the occasional overseas tour. At least four bands of this sort flourish on Manhattan Island. One is led by the trumpeter Howard McGhee, another by the pianist-composer Duke Pearson, another by the trumpeter Clark Terry ('We brought the big band back to Harlem,' he proudly boasts), and a fourth by the trumpeter Thad Jones (brother of Hank and Elvin) in tandem with the drummer Mel Lewis. (Jones and Lewis had the idea of running a band together at the end of the 1950s, when they were playing in Gerry Mulligan's Concert Jazz Band.) The concept has spread to Europe too. Neil Ardley organized the New Jazz Orchestra in London almost as a way of letting British jazz composers hear what their scores sounded like. On the other side of the Channel a band was formed under the joint leadership of an American drummer, Kenny Clarke, one of the pioneers of bebop, and the Belgian pianist-composer Francy Boland, in which Europeans like the Swedish trombonist Ake Persson, Yugoslav trumpeter Dusko Gojkovic and the British saxophonists Ronnie Scott, Derek Humble and Tony Coe sat beside such American expatriates as Johnny Griffin and Sahib Shihab.

But all the bands mentioned so far—except, in a mild way, for the New Jazz Orchestra—never stray far from the traditional line-up, with sections of trumpets, trombones, saxophones and rhythm instruments, their first necessity a lead trumpeter with lips of steel and a drummer who never drags. Yet the 1950s and 1960s saw small group jazz loosen up, demanding greater empathy between individual players. A few big bands, mostly assembled for records or other special occasions, moved that way too. In New York the Jazz Composers' Orchestra and Charlie Haden's Liberation Music have personnels which overlap, but Haden's band is politically committed, something of a rarity in jazz, Carla Bley's arrangements of Spanish Civil War songs getting played alongside pieces dedicated to Ché and other revolutionary heroes or events, yet without po-faced solemnity.

In Britain the London Jazz Composers' Orchestra, the brain child of bassist Barry Guy, pursues a policy akin to that of its namesake in New York, performing works constructed around the new generation of free jazz players. Britain also has the Brotherhood

of Breath, using a nucleus of African musicians, and at its best when playing the kwela-tinged scores of its leader Chris McGregor, who tosses a theme from trombones to saxophones to trumpets with the nonchalance of an expert demonstrating the three-card trick.

The pop influence looms larger in a couple of other British bands: both Mike Gibbs's Orchestra and the Mike Westbrook Concert Band throw in entire rock rhythm sections (eight-to-a-bar drumming, plus electric and bass guitars, complete with feed-back), while Westbrook often features a light-show as well. But the father of mixed media in jazz must be Sun Ra, born Sonny Bourke, a pianist ('I studied music under Nature's God, then with Mrs. Lula Randolph of Washington, D.C.') who once played with Fletcher Henderson, afterwards led his own band at Chicago's Grand Terrace, and moved to New York in 1960. With his Myth-Science Arkestra, Sun Ra gives concerts which fuse space-fiction, occultism and the pantomime tradition with the musical and theatrical techniques of black show-biz. His music is more graspable than his gnomic sayings ('Everything is everything and outside of that is nothing'), pastiches of Duke Ellington, Debussy and Don Redman co-existing with avant-garde solos and the leader's pummeling of piano and Moog synthesizer, all of it making more sense than a dead-pan listing suggests. The Arkestra sports a fire-eater too, something Glenn Miller would certainly have drawn the line at.

*Below* Woody Herman. *Left* Four Ellington reedmen: Paul Gonsalves, Jimmy Hamilton, Johnny Hodges, Russell Procope.

WOODY

Right *Aboard the Count Basie coach:*
*Fip Ricard, Al Aarons, Marshall Royal,*
*Henry Coker, Charlie Fowlkes, Bill*
*Hughes, Sonny Payne, Sonny Cohn.*
Below *Stan Kenton.* Far right *Duke*
*Ellington's Harry Carney with the*
*London Philharmonic Orchestra.*

Right *Count Basie saxophonists Bobby Plater, Marshall Royal, Lockjaw Davis.* Far right *Kenny Clarke-Francy Boland Orchestra: (l to r) Tony Coe, Johnny Griffin, Kenny Clarke, Derek Humble, Kenny Clare, Ronnie Scott.* Bottom left *Duke Ellington Orchestra rehearsing with the London Philharmonic Orchestra: (l to r) Ellington, Paul Gonsalves, Jimmy Hamilton, John Lamb, Johnny Hodges, Cootie Williams, Lawrence Brown, Russell Procope.* Bottom right *The Mike Westbrook Band: (l to r) Westbrook, Harry Miller, John Surman, Alan Jackson, Mike Osborne, Dave Holdsworth, Alan Skidmore, Malcolm Griffiths, Bernie Livings, Paul Rutherford.*

# Common Market Jazzman

It started like a science-fiction story. The old farmhouse with shuttered windows, eerie sounds heard late at night, Flemish-speaking villagers whispering and wondering. Yet the events which took place during the autumn of 1969 in the Belgian village of St Pierre Capel, about thirty miles outside Brussels, could be explained quite rationally. Two American musicians, Barre Phillips and Stu Martin, had joined forces with an Englishman, John Surman, to form a group they called The Trio. But before taking on a single job they needed to get the music right. The solution was three months in the oak-beamed farmhouse, playing, talking, listening. 'In London I lived in an atmosphere of getting something together for tomorrow,' says John Surman. 'My ambition always was for us to go off and damned well play day after day. So we did. With no plans, no special ideas—it was hopeless! But in the end we found out what we *all* wanted to do. Which was better than if I'd started rehearsing a batch of my tunes and Stu had come up with a couple of his.'

The Trio has toured all over Europe, creating jazz which is free yet closely-knit, very decidedly a collaboration between three unique musicians. The backgrounds of the two Americans were conventional enough by jazz standards, the kind of *curricula vitae* to be found on the sleeve of almost any jazz LP. Stu Martin first came to Europe in 1959, as Quincy Jones's drummer, had worked in the Count Basie, Duke Ellington and Maynard Ferguson bands, and been one-fourth of Gary Burton's original quartet. Barre Phillips, a string bass virtuoso, straddled two musical camps: as sideman with Archie Shepp, Jimmy Giuffre and George Russell, as soloist with Leonard Bernstein and the New York Philharmonic.

Left *The Trio on-stage with John Surman at front.* Right *Bassist Barre Phillips.*

John Surman was different. With his Devonshire accent and countryman's plod, nobody could look less like a jazz musician, let alone a great one. Yet he happens to be the best baritone saxophonist in the world (he's no slouch with the soprano saxophone either), important not just because of the originality of his ideas but also as

a technician; nobody else is so expert at playing harmonics, those freak high notes; nobody else has a range stretching from the lowest note reachable on a baritone saxophone to the highest an alto can climb to. Not that Surman sits around furbishing his talents. 'I don't practise at all,' he says. 'When I was at college I did some fairly hard work on the clarinet before I took my Finals, but just practising by itself means nothing to me. What I am interested in is developing my relationship to the instrument. That's something you can only do by playing— and playing with other people.'

John Surman is probably the finest jazz musician that Britain has produced; certainly the best since Victor Feldman, an infant prodigy who actually got

better, slipped off to the United States. But like all British jazzmen Surman faced the problem of finding enough work. 'The trouble is that you keep on playing to the same people all the time,' he says. 'Everyone has heard everybody. So the people who make it in London have always got to be just discovered, just coming up.' Surman himself spent a long time coming up. When John Coltrane, a particular hero, visited Britain in 1961 the young student could not afford the fare to London to hear him. That same year he started playing with the band Mike Westbrook ran at Plymouth Art School; when Westbrook moved to London Surman went with him. His name began getting around but by 1969 he felt the need to stretch once again.

That was why The Trio was formed, why the Belgian farmhouse was rented, why, soon afterwards, John and Janet Surman moved to Paris. By 1971, however, a blend of nostalgia for English beer and alarm over the French cost of living brought them back to Britain. 'From a working point of view,' Surman explains, 'it doesn't really matter where our home is. You see, tours like those the Trio does last for 25 or 26 days on the trot, with us normally playing somewhere new every night. So the only difference living in Britain makes is that the journey to the first gig is a bit longer.' Yet sometimes that journey is longer than usual. In the summer of 1970 Surman toured Japan with a band that included Francy Boland, Daniel Humair, Karin Krog, Albert Mangelsdorff, Niels Henning Orsted-Pedersen and Jean-Luc Ponty, all of them 'Down Beat' European Poll Winners. But that kind of moving round—especially in Europe—looks like becoming more common-place.

'There's no reason why your musical associates shouldn't live hundreds of miles away', says Surman. 'European jazz is like a large, spread-out family. Because of the spaciousness nobody need worry that someone is pinching his special gigs—which isn't true of a small, more static scene like London. Continental radio and TV producers have more money to put on shows by artists they like. And more people read what the jazz critics write—they're actually influenced by it, too.' John Surman is far from being the first British jazz musician to earn most of his living in Europe. But while he and other British players are free to wander all over the Continent, the Musicians' Union prevents foreign jazzmen from performing in Britain without a carefully organized exchange. Barre Phillips and Stu Martin were able to tour Britain with The Trio in 1970 because of a complicated swap which sent a pop group, The Pink Floyd, to the United States. But eventually rules and regulations have to catch up with the way people actually behave. For that reason, John Surman is important politically as well as aesthetically, a shining example of an up-and-coming breed—the Common Market jazzman.

Below *The Trio's drummer, Stu Martin.*
Right *John Surman.*

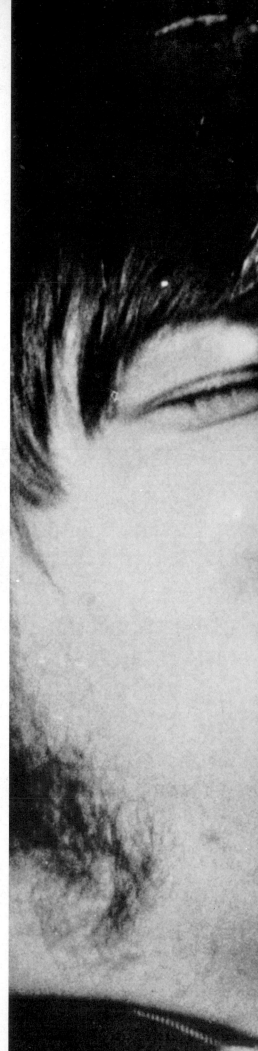

# Americans in Europe

Moscow was the improbable setting for the first meeting between two of the greatest New Orleans musicians, Sidney Bechet and Tommy Ladnier. The year was 1926. Bechet, billed as 'The Talking Saxophone', was there with Bennie Peyton's band. He wanted a camera in order to photograph the Muscovite scene and heard one was being offered for sale by a trumpet player in Sam Wooding's orchestra, also touring the Soviet Union. Thirty-six years before the US State Department sent Benny Goodman behind the Iron Curtain, that meeting is a reminder of just how early and how busily jazz musicians started globe-trotting. For example, during the same year in which Bechet ran across Ladnier the pianist Teddy Weatherford pulled out of Erskine Tate's Little Symphony at Chicago's Vendome Theatre; after sailing to the Orient he led bands in Singapore, Manila, Shanghai and other Somerset Maugham locales before dying of cholera in Calcutta 29 years later.

But Europe was the main stamping ground for that first generation of jazz missionaries. Not that many were fired by the desire to proselytize; they simply found work easier to get there, especially during the Depression. And as the Twenties melted into the Thirties they began realizing that Europeans took them and their music more seriously than Americans did, treating the jazzman as an artist rather than a hired entertainer. For black musicians there was also the discovery that, especially in France and the Latin countries, their colour was no longer a drawback; indeed, black jazzmen were positively fashionable. All of which helps to explain the exodus from the United States of quite a few distinguished performers. At the very time when he was the most admired saxophonist in jazz, Coleman Hawkins chose to spend five years— from 1934 to 1939—working all over the Continent, often having to put up with sloppy rhythm sections but always acclaimed, always in demand.

Many of the musicians who came stayed on. Bill Coleman, a trumpeter whose quicksilver style anticipated the beboppers' expertise, would probably have enjoyed more renown—reputations,

Below *Albert Nicholas.* Right *Johnny Griffin in Trafalgar Square.*

after all, still depended on American exposure—had he not visited Paris with Lucky Millinder's Orchestra in 1933. Two years later he went back, and has lived there ever since, apart from a spell in Egypt and the war-years in the United States. Sidney Bechet's case is not so surprising, for he grew up in the Frenchified atmosphere of Creole New Orleans, after which Paris seemed like a second home. He spent the last eight years of his life

there—from 1951 to 1959—and even had a street named in his honour. Another of the most fluent New Orleans reed players, Albert Nicholas, moved to Paris in 1953. Thirteen years later, Selmer, the French instrument firm, presented him with a gold-keyed clarinet to celebrate fifty years of earning his living from jazz. ('You know, all the time I was in the States,' said Nicholas, 'I didn't even get so much as a reed.')

Albert Nicholas and Bill Coleman still live and work in Paris. So does Mezz Mezzrow, although he performs in public less frequently. A white clarinettist who spiked beer for Al Capone in Chicago, and later heard his name become a synonym for the choicest Harlem reefers ('A mighty mezz but not too strong,' sang Rosetta Howard in *If You're A Viper*), Mezzrow also wrote the confessional 'Really The Blues', not quite in the De Quincey class but a vivid guide to where the action was before Charlie Parker took over and the hipsters moved in. Parker's widow, Chan, is now married to the alto saxophonist Phil Woods, another white expatriate, who claims to have played more jazz since he arrived in Europe in 1968 than he ever had the chance to do in America— including eleven years of session work. Woods tours with his European Rhythm Machine, comprising a British pianist and a French bassist and drummer.

Mostly, however, the expatriates are black. As Dexter Gordon says, 'You're not the Invisible Man. People see you here.' Gordon has settled in Copenhagen, takes at least one sauna bath a week and blows his tenor saxophone all over Norway, Sweden and Denmark. Ben Webster, owner of the lushest saxophone sound in jazz, has also been living in Scandinavia. Among other American jazzmen who now spend most of their working time in Europe are Benny Bailey, Don Cherry, Kenny Clarke, Kenny Drew, Stan Getz, Johnny Griffin, Hampton Hawes, Philly Joe Jones, Jimmy

Raney, Sahib Shihab, Idress Sulieman, Jimmy Woode—but a list would take up a whole page. Not long ago an entire community of musicians flew into Paris, black avant-gardists who include Rosoe Mitchell, Joseph Jarman, Anthony Braxton, Lester Bowie and Malachi Favors, all founder-members of the Chicago-based Association for the Advancement of Creative Musicians. Some arrivals stay for a while, then go back. Others, like the pixie-faced tenor saxophonist Don Byas, have been around so long that they announce tune-titles with a French accent.

Perhaps the most surprising ex-patriates have been a couple of piano-playing blues singers. Surprising, because while jazz is as international in character as European art music, blues still seem functional, rooted in black American society. The first man to soften up Europe for blues was Big Bill Broonzy, who toured just after the war, shrewdly announcing the demise of every other bluesman who might spoil the market. ('Sleepy John Estes? Man, that was such a shame. I was at his funeral.') But nothing could hold back the flood of blues artists who crossed the Atlantic during the 1950s and 1960s. The two who have stayed are Memphis Slim and Champion Jack Dupree. Helped by the royalties from *Every Day I Have The Blues*, Slim (his real name is Peter Chatman) lives in the 16th *arrondisement* and drives round Paris in a Rolls Royce Silver Cloud. Britain, too fussy about labour permits and union approval for most American jazzmen, has become home for Dupree, who learned to play boogie-woogie on New Orleans' Rampart Street, boxed well enough— at lightweight—nearly to become a Championship contender, and now lives in the gritty hinterland between Bradford and Halifax. Next door is his Yorkshire-born father-in-law, who acts as manager and drives him to jobs in a maroon Austin Cambridge—bluesmen tend to be status-conscious—with curtains in the rear windows and CHAMPION JACK DUPREE—BLUES PIANIST OF NEW ORLEANS stencilled in gold along the side.

Top left *Tenor saxophonist Ben Webster (r) with New Orleans drummer Zutty Singleton (l).* Top right *Alto saxophonist Phil Woods.* Bottom left *Trumpeter Bill Coleman in the studio (his wife Lily is in the background).* Bottom right *Kenny Clarke lecturing at a Drum Clinic in London.*

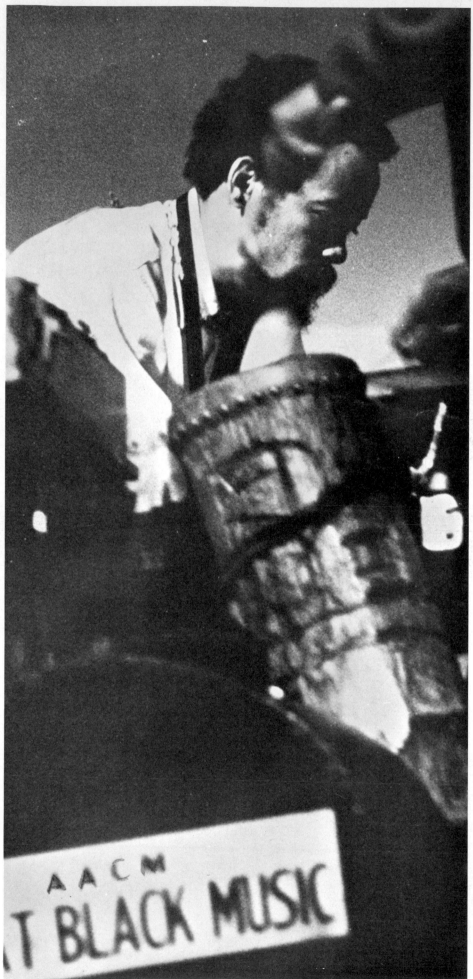

Above *Tenor saxophonist Dexter Gordon.* Right *Joseph Jarman, one of the members of the Chicago-based Association for the Advancement of Creative Musicians who moved to Paris.* Far right *Tenor saxophonist Don Byas has lived in Europe since 1946.*

# Jazz Fusions

Nothing does an art or a nation so much good as letting foreigners in. Chaucer importing French verse-forms, Picasso's obsession with African masks, the conjunction of Indian and European in Spanish colonial church-building: all are shining examples of cultural miscegenation. Jazz itself resulted from that sort of coupling, a marriage between the music of Africans transported to America and the Anglo-Saxon hymns of the slave-owners. Africa, in fact, lies only just below the surface of most pre-jazz forms: the call-and-response pattern of work-songs and gospel music, the riffs in ragtime, the flattened notes of the blues scale. Yet from that conspiracy of events, those separate cultural strands, came a music with its own identity, its own way of going about things.

During the seventy or so years of its fully-fledged life, jazz has affected and been affected by other sorts of music. A love-hate relationship with pop has resulted in dance bands watering down jazz techniques and jazz soloists improvising on pop songs. And ever since George Gershwin sat at the piano in New York's Aeolian Hall, one February day in 1921, and performed his *Rhapsody In Blue* with Paul Whiteman's orchestra, a few musicians have been eager to push jazz inside classical structures and to write for strings as well as brass and reeds. Flirtations with Latin-American idioms began even further back and were very much an American preoccupation. Right from the start, a good deal of New Orleans music had what Jelly Roll Morton used to call 'the Spanish tinge', partly a legacy of the city being in either French or Spanish hands until the Louisiana Purchase of 1803. Duke Ellington recorded *Maori*, a jazz rumba, in 1931, a year which also saw Louis Armstrong score a hit with *The Peanut Vendor*.

But before the Second World War most Latin-American orchestras were like Xavier Cugat's, decidedly on the sweet side. The influx of Puerto Ricans into New York during the 1940s helped to change this, for the newcomers liked rumba bands to be much hotter, much more dramatic. So America was introduced to the fiercer music of orchestras like those led by Machito

and Perez Prado. Mambo records made in Havana deliberately mixed Cuban rhythms with jazz-type scoring for brass and reeds, a formula quickly taken over by Dizzy Gillespie. In fact, most of the fusions involving Latin-American idioms were first tried out by the beboppers. Almost the only development since then has been bossa nova, gracefully, if sometimes monotonously, combining the melodic lines of modern jazz with the swaying rhythms of the Brazilian samba.

Right *South African in London: Chris McGregor.* Below *John Mayer.*

It was in the 1960s that musicians of all kinds became properly aware of Oriental music, especially Indian. They observed it had qualities which were lacking in European music, characteristics which might even help to solve the problem of what to do once the chords have run out. But as well as using a raga instead of an harmonic sequence, Indian music is much concerned with space; it also exploits rhythms more complex than Westerners are used to, and its soloists will often split a single note into five or six tinier ones. Not much expertise is needed to

discover affinities between, say, Miles Davis or John Coltrane improvising on a scale and an Indian sitar or sarod player improvising on a raga. Indeed, Davis and Coltrane even began using clusters of notes, achieving a festooning effect, quite unlike the melodic unfolding found in most earlier jazz solos. Coltrane in full flight could make a single number last for anything up to half an hour, the string bass thrumming like a tambura, Elvin Jones's cross-rhythms rivalling those of a tabla player.

There were other, perhaps more obvious ways of doing it. Indo-Jazz Fusions, a double quartet led by the West Indian alto saxophonist, Joe Harriott, and the Indian violinist and composer, John Mayer, went in for face-to-face confrontation, with Indian and jazz musicians playing alongside one another. If the Indian half tended to dominate, it was because most of the pieces were based on ragas and the jazz percussionist usually got upstaged by the tabla player. For a time pop musicians were also fascinated by Eastern techniques; Ravi Shankar even performed at a Californian pop festival. But pop music did little more than copy the sound, that wiry twang of the sitar, while jazz, whether it was John Coltrane or Indo-Jazz Fusions, took over the structures and actual working methods. Sometimes, just to complicate matters, there have been three-way fusions, like the work of Amancio D'Silva, a guitarist born in Goa, who blends jazz with both Indian and Portuguese music.

Britain was a natural headquarters for this kind of experimenting. The British Raj only crumbled in 1947; up to then India had been part of an Empire which centred on London, an Empire whose territories—bright pink in pre-war atlases—also took in vast stretches of Africa. Those links remained after the Empire turned into the Commonwealth. Just as John Mayer headed for London from Calcutta and Joe Harriott from the West Indies, the drummer Guy Warren—'Guy Warren of Ghana', as his passport puts it—flew in from West Africa. And in 1965 a young white South African, Chris McGregor, brought over his Blue Notes, all-black except for himself, a band

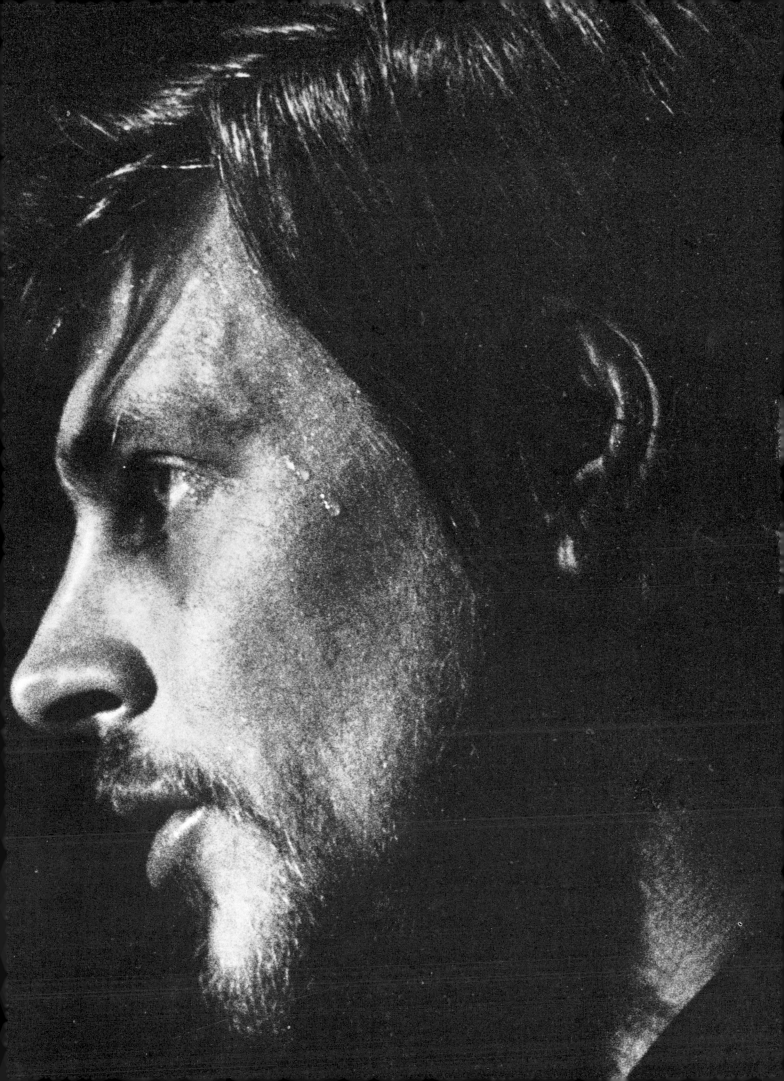

which gradually ventured further and further into avant-garde territory yet went on reflecting the sound and spirit of kwela. This was even truer of McGregor's large bands, culminating in The Brotherhood of Breath, and of Spear, a small group made up of McGregor sidemen and led by his drummer, Louis Moholo. (On the other hand, Osibisa, a later arrival—four West Africans, three West Indians—remains essentially a drum band, its music tilting a different way.) Kwela is the South African counterpart of West African high-life, big city music, using plenty of sweet, fat riffs and filled with the over-riding sound of saxophones. (Most of the musicians start on penny whistles as children, moving on to alto saxophones when they grow up.) In a way it is the most understandable fusion of all, African music responding to the impact of American jazz, almost a classic example of the wanderer returning home.

Left *Guy Warren of Ghana.* Top *Joe Harriott (alto sax), Amancio D'Silva (guitar).* Bottom *Dudu Pukwane.* Right *South African drummer Louis Moholo.*

*Avant-garde jazz at Cambridge: (l to r) unknown trumpet and saxophone, Barre Phillips, Mongesi Feza, Johnny Dyanni, Dudu Pukwane, Chris McGregor, John Tchicai, Trevor Watts, Louis Moholo.*

# Free and Far Out

April may be the cruellest month and June the sexiest, but October is the revolutionary's choice. Typically enough, it was in October 1964, at the Cellar Cafe on 91st Street, near Broadway, a handily conspiratorial address, that New Yorkers were invited to 'The October Revolution In Jazz'— that was how the posters, not so conspiratorial, put it—four days of music-making by Paul Bley, John Tchicai, Don Heckman, Milford Graves, Ed Summerlin, Giuseppi Logan, David Izenzon, Joe Scianni and scores of other established or aspiring avant-gardists, all aiming to prove that the organiser, Bill Dixon, a trumpet-playing composer, was right when he

announced that 'the new music is not ahead of the people—all it needs is a chance to be heard'. It was the public surfacing of the young and not-so-young musicians who had been emancipated by Ornette Coleman and Cecil Taylor. Up to this time they had mostly played for one another and for friends in artists' lofts on the lower East Side or in Greenwich Village coffee shops. Now they ventured into the open.

Not all were even near-geniuses. Some were spectacularly untalented, adept only at rapping on about the uniqueness of their emotions, and how even the flimsiest disciplines seemed like a prison. Yet as well as the

charlatans and the innocents there were genuine creators, but they differed from earlier jazzmen in being much more exclusive. Swing-period musicians had happily jammed alongside New Orleans veterans, beboppers sat in with players from the Ellington or Basie bands, all accepting a single common denominator: the chord sequence. Now it was a case of every group for itself, with empathy between performers every bit as vital as knowing the musical compass-points. According to Cecil Taylor's sidemen, it took three years of steady rehearsal for them properly to get to grips with their leader's music. When Norman Granz invited John Coltrane to tour with 'Jazz At The Philharmonic', the saxophonist declined to do it unless his quartet could work with him.

Ironically enough, Ornette Coleman did not blow a single note in public during 1964, but stayed in his flat, practising the trumpet and violin, preparing for his reappearance the following year. Two of his sidemen, Don Cherry and the drummer Billy Higgins, were working with Sonny Rollins, who had recently taken a long sabbatical himself. Despite being reared as a bebopper, Rollins has always preferred to develop themes rather than improvise above harmonies, a predilection that made him more *simpatico* to young musicians than most of his contemporaries were. In any case, Rollins's saxophone style was a prime influence upon one of the most radical of the new players, Albert Ayler. Like so many black jazzmen, Ayler got his early training in rhythm-and-blues bands. Called up by the US Army, he came to Europe, where he sat in at Paris jazz clubs and stayed on for a while after his discharge. Already his music was provoking strong reactions. 'I remember one night in Stockholm,' he told the American jazz critic, Nat Hentoff, 'I started to play what was in my soul, but the promoter pulled me off the stage.'

Ayler described bebop as being at once too constricting and too obvious. 'It was like humming along with Mitch Miller,' he said, 'it was *too* simple.' However, the band he co-led with his brother, the trumpeter Donald Ayler, not only played marches in the old style but what seemed remarkably like the dirges—slow, lamenting, dissonant—heard at New Orleans funerals. A British critic, W. A. Baldwin, even suggests that the sounds Albert Ayler dragged from his instrument had something in common with the unusual timbres and effects which New Orleans brass players went in for; the trouble, Baldwin says, was that jazz fans were used to hearing trumpeters and trombonists do this sort of thing, but not saxophone players. Undoubtedly Ayler's early notoriety rested on these bizarre noises, excruciating for people who thought fixed pitch and a consistent tone integral to music; young players quickly caught on, however, adapting Ayler's manner for their own purposes. In other ways Ayler seemed relatively old-fashioned, mostly sticking to straight-ahead 4/4 time, and, just like Ornette Coleman, just like Sonny Rollins, building his solos round motifs. Towards the end of his life—he was 34 when the New York police fished his body out of the East River in November 1970—Ayler had come almost full-circle, merging his abrasive style inside the formula of black pop music, fulfilling a prophecy made by Leroi Jones—dramatist, poet, sometime jazz critic and Black Power spokesman—that r-and-b and the new

Black Music would join together.

The violence inside the playing of Albert Ayler and other black avant-gardists has been rationalized as a reflection of racial anger. Sometimes it is. Ayler once said he felt that on the tenor saxophone 'you could get out all the feelings of the ghetto'. Archie Shepp, whose playing oscillates between a romanticism distilled from Coleman Hawkins and Ben Webster, and a defiant, more akimbo style, might agree with him, even though he has called the instrument 'a Freudian symbol, a killer of women'. Shepp would also go along with Ayler's statement, 'Jazz is Jim Crow', for he thinks of himself as playing not jazz but Black Music, which by implication forms part of the black man's struggle

*Tenor saxophonists who play Black Music.* Above *Pharoah Sanders, once a member of the John Coltrane group.* Right *Archie Shepp, spokesman as well as soloist.*

for identity in America. Yet this has never stopped Shepp or other black avant-gardists from employing white musicians. For a long time, Shepp's trombonist was Roswell Rudd, once a member of Eli's Chosen Seven, a white Dixieland group, and a soloist able to conjure up a pugnacious lyricism akin to Joe Nanton's or Dickie Wells's, while Ayler used a white violinist, Michael Sampson, who would warm up off-stage with a Bach sonata. White bassists have been heavily in demand, perhaps because

the new jazz suddenly needed classical techniques that ordinary jazz bassists had never learned or bothered about. So David Izenzon and Charlie Haden have worked with Ornette Coleman, and Gary Peacock, Bill Folwell and Alan Silva with Albert Ayler. Plenty of other white performers were active in the new music, men like the soprano saxophonist Steve Lacy, who had moved straight out of Sidney Bechet's group to work with Cecil Taylor ('Just play,' Taylor replied when Lacy asked what he should do), and, from an earlier generation, the saxophonist and clarinettist Jimmy Giuffre, who wrote *Four Brothers* for Woody Herman's orchestra and in the 1950s had tried playing without a rhythm section, just tapping his foot on the floor.

After Ornette Coleman moved from Los Angeles to New York, most avant-garde activity revolved around Manhattan Island. Yet there were tremors elsewhere, notably in Chicago, a city where nothing significant had happened—from a jazz standpoint, that is—since the action-packed 1920s. During the 1950s Chicago not only spawned a new kind of urban blues but witnessed the experimentings—part musical, part mystical—of Sun Ra and his loyal henchmen, before they shifted to New York in 1960. Five years later a group of black Chicago avant-gardists, including Richard Abrams, Joseph Jarman, Roscoe Mitchell and Anthony Braxton, founded the Association for the Advancement of Creative Musicians, mixing a regard for tradition—the violinist Leroy Jenkins hero-worshipped Stuff Smith and Eddie South, the trumpeter Lester Bowie blew harmonica more funkily than most bluesmen—with an involvement in sound for its own sake. Braxton's declaration that he is searching for instruments 'that are not concerned with actual fixed pitches, instruments with whirls of sound in them', helps to explain why, as well as using conventional saxophones, trumpets and clarinets, the AACM also falls back on such curiosa as slide whistles, kazoos, a koto and kelp horn, even an inverted frying pan.

In 1969 the nucleus of the AACM took a trip to Paris. Other avant-gardists had already been traipsing round Europe, among them Don Cherry, who started out copying Clifford Brown but developed his own style during the years with Ornette Coleman. The saxophonist John Tchicai, half-Danish, half-Negro, returned to Copenhagen and organized a 17-piece orchestra, Cadentia Nova Danica. In any case, European musicians were well abreast of events in America. The West Indian, Joe Harriott, had even been playing his own brand of free jazz around London in 1960. Two musicians who met in the Royal Air Force, the drummer John Stevens and the alto saxophonist

Trevor Watts, formed the Spontaneous Music Ensemble in 1965, playing at a tiny London club theatre where the clinking of glasses at the bar could be heard above the music. This unlikely venue became the first headquarters of the early British avant-gardists, including Chris McGregor's all-African Blue Notes, with Dudu Pukwana's alto saxophone slicing the smoky air and Mongesi Feza high-stepping like a circus pony as he played his pocket trumpet.

Some European approaches edge closer to 'straight' avant-garde practices, with performers from the two areas occasionally overlapping. First off the mark in Germany was the trumpeter Manfred Schoof, leading a group which contained the pianist-composer, Alexander von Schlippenbach. The British drummer, Tony Oxley, devises graphic scores calling for certain kinds of dynamics, certain ranges of sound, but several of his musicians, among them the saxophonist Evan Parker and the guitarist Derek Bailey, hold out for total unpredictability. So does the German saxophonist Peter Brotzman—'his moustache like Bismarck's, his sound like Odin's'—and his bassist Peter Kowald, the Swiss pianist Irene Schweitzer and the drummer Pierre Favre, and various Dutch players active in the Instant Composers' Pool, including the percussionist Han Bennink, the pianist Misha Mengelberg and the saxophonist Willem Breuker. The European avant-garde, in fact, has a character of its own, no longer primarily Afro-American, certainly separate from free jazz as played in the United States. 'The American approach seems very diffuse,' says Evan Parker. 'Musicians on the Continent have a greater sense of purpose. They're more rigorous, not so eclectic.'

Left *Halfway through the 1960s Albert Ayler upset many jazz fans with the violence of his playing, the bizarre sounds he conjured from the saxophone.* Right *Front-line of the Archie Shepp Quintet, with Shepp (tenor sax) flanked by his two trombonists: Grachan Moncur III (l), Roswell Rudd (r).* Top left *Drummer John Stevens, who with alto saxophonist Trevor Watts pioneered free jazz in Britain in the mid-1960s.* Top right *Sun Ra, Chicago pianist, composer and bandleader who moved to New York and specialises in blending avant-garde jazz with occultism, science-fiction and black show business.*

# Miles Davis

Father figures abounded before Sigmund Freud started plumbing the id. They will go on being needed long after the last analyst sells off his couch. Art-forms require them just as much as people do, usually opting for innovators who are also guardians of tradition, creative yet holding a watching brief for the past. Louis Armstrong was the first, then Duke Ellington, but Charlie Parker had to die before being turned into a guru. To suggest that Miles Davis has now taken over—from Ellington more than anybody else—will stir up protest, but only from jazz fans who are blind to both his innate conservatism and his revolutionary fervour. The dress-style may have changed, 'hippy' instead of Italian, the sounds become startlingly up-to-date, yet Davis's playing has kept its identity. The protégé of Charlie Parker, the apostle of coolness, the spiky jazz-rock star: all developed within a single, comprehensible pattern.

At the start of the 1950s Miles Davis was becoming famous for his allusiveness, his understatement, the way he made a single note do the work of ten. In 1949 he had collaborated with the arranger Gil Evans on a set of records that changed the sound and shape of small band jazz. Eight years later the two men got together for a series of LPs—*Miles Ahead* is the best-known—in which Evans supplied ravishing textures and Davis's flugel-horn a tiptoeing curiosity. But by then Charlie Parker was dead and somehow Davis seemed more confident, freer to stand on his own two feet. His next step was to help jazz get rid of the tight chord sequences that Parker had revelled in, replacing them with a lightly-poised modality, epitomised in *Kind of Blue*, an LP made in 1959 when John Coltrane was working with Davis's Sextet. After that the trumpeter marked time, happy to play the ballads and 'standards' which people asked for, until halfway through the 1960s, he suddenly sprinted forward again.

Up to this point Miles Davis had mostly hired musicians of his own generation. By 1965, however, his group was full of young men, eager to hurry him into brand-new territory. His pianist, Herbie Hancock, and saxophonist, Wayne Shorter, wrote

oblique, often vestigial themes, Davis responded by studding his solos with clusters of notes that struck the ear like separate images, the conception pointilliste instead of linear. He was manifestly the same musician who, a decade earlier, had introduced into jazz a new sensibility, a quality of introspection akin to T. S. Eliot's early poems or the novels of Proust; yet playing that once suggested a man reading aloud from his diary now took on an unfamiliar abrasiveness, cutting more than soothing, the famous Harmon mute used to threaten rather than cajole.

Below *Miles Davis in action.* Right *The Miles Davis Quintet with Chick Corea (piano) and British-born Dave Holland (bass).*

There were other changes too. Davis's new drummer, Tony Williams, began dictating shifts of mood as well as tempo. Some numbers had no proper solos, just restless activity below the horns from piano, bass and drums. By the end of the 1960s Chick Corea was making his electric piano sound like a spinet at one moment, a guitarist's fuzzbox the next, distorting tone like an electronic composer, while the string bass began to be ousted by the bass guitar. The quintet's approach was vehement, a night of long knives without the blood, a family turmoil, uneasy but intimate. Anyone who went along expecting Davis to noodle his way through *Green Dolphin Street* was in for a very rude surprise. The *morbidezza* was still there but the trumpeter had followed the opposite path to Louis Armstrong, renouncing the virtuoso's role, immersing himself within the group.

Not that his actual command of the trumpet was ever particularly impressive Dizzy Gillespie and Davis's near-contemporaries, Fats Navarro and Clifford Brown, all possessed much finer techniques. What Miles Davis does have, however, is the capacity to illuminate rather than explain, an ability to hint at profundities just out of ear-shot. The gift had been there all the time, even when, fumbling a little, he recorded *Embraceable You* with Charlie Parker. It was still there, hedged in by electronic shimmering,

when he played at Fillmore East and took over from Tiny Tim at the Isle of Wight Pop Festival. It is one of the reasons why jazz writers feel a need to drape him with fancy similes—'a man walking on eggshells', or Whitney Balliett likening his sound to angora.

The life-style is important too. Four times a week Miles Davis drives his battleship-grey Lamborghini to Bobby Gleason's Gym in the Bronx, pulls on a pair of bright blue trunks and works out in the boxing ring. A vegetarian, non-smoker and non-drinker, Davis does 40 push-ups and 40 sit-ups every day. The same self-discipline came to his aid in 1954, when, hooked on heroin, he took a cold-turkey cure, locking himself in a room and staring at the ceiling for nearly two weeks. Lacking bonhomie but with a voice as gravelly as Louis Armstrong's (legend has it that a throat operation went awry), Miles Davis excels at the sharp brush-off. But there are inconsistencies. He may have spotted the worthwhileness of Jimi Hendrix and Bob Dylan early on, yet some of his judgements have been fallible. 'He plays like somebody was standing on his foot,' Davis once said of Eric Dolphy. And while scoffing at the very notion of white musicians being able to swing, he continued to work and record with two Britishers, bassist Dave Holland and guitarist John McLaughlin. His get-out might be that playing alongside blacks transformed their sound.

Testiness of this sort has roots in

the past. 'About the first thing I can remember as a little boy was a white man running me down on the street hollering "Nigger! Nigger!",' Miles Davis told a Playboy interviewer. Yet he grew up in a well-to-do home in St Louis, where his father was a dentist and landowner; he never went hungry or scuffled for a bed. Today he must be one of the wealthiest jazzmen alive. But without paradoxes life would seem tiresome, and Davis's virtues and shortcomings interlocked. Already well into his forties, the trumpeter might have rested on his laurels, easing up like Duke Ellington, re-enacting his past like Monk or Dizzy Gillespie. Instead he has chosen to go on taking risks. There is no parallel in jazz for a musician of his stature and maturity passing through so many phases. Just as James Joyce wrote every book a different way, Miles Davis persists in bewitching or bemusing his admirers, yet without sacrificing identity. His blend of curiosity and tradition, his zest for using the past as a launching-pad, give him authority over the young and forces respect from the elderly. It might be called a recipe for the ideal father figure.

Left *During his stay with Miles Davis, saxophonist Wayne Shorter wrote many compositions for the Quintet.* Right *British guitarist John McLaughlin has recorded with Davis.*

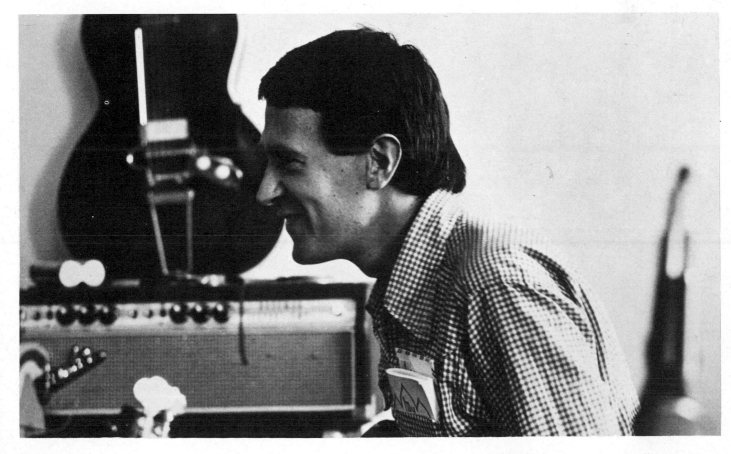

Left *Two moods of Miles.*
Below *Herbie Hancock, pianist with the
Miles Davis Quintet from 1963 to 1969
(he also wrote the tune* Watermelon
Man, *popularized by Mongo
Santamaria).* Overleaf left *A thoughtful
Miles Davis.* Overleaf right *Ron Carter,
bassist with Davis from 1963 to 1969.*

# The Scene Today

Jazz is the toughest music around. It needs to be. Life has usually been difficult for jazzmen too dedicated to compromise or take the easy way out. Still slightly out of step with the Establishment, a bit respectable and long in the tooth for the trendy and teen-aged, jazz holds the shaky middle ground. Jazz musicians have to cope with an artist's responsibilities and hang-ups while remaining second-class citizens culturally, often racially too. Ornette Coleman and Charlie Haden have been given Guggenheim fellowships but otherwise the American academic world studiously ignores the only authentically American art form. When Duke Ellington, at the age of sixty-six, received a Pulitzer prize citation in 1965 for 'long-term achievement', it was turned down without explanation by the advisory board. ('Fate's being kind to me; Fate doesn't want me to be too famous too soon,' was Ellington's suave but dry response.) In Europe things are marginally better. State-run TV and radio stations sponsor weekends of jazz, even commission jazz works. The Arts Council of Great Britain regularly doles out bursaries. Yet the business of being a jazz musician stays hazardous, fraught with problems.

It is not simply a matter of pioneers being rebuffed. At any given moment the bulk of practising musicians are neither avant-gardists nor revivalists but occupied in working the seam of the last revolution but one. Performers moving most diligently round the concert or club circuits are people like Oscar Peterson, his virtuosity obvious even to audiences hazy about the difference between a blues and a ballad; Stan Getz, whose cooing versions of bossa-nova melodies made him a household name but who refuses to be type-cast, just as he scorns falling back on a cliché; Bill Evans, sometimes accused of playing 'cocktail music' yet a pianist who can, in the deftest, most subtle ways, give a theme new harmonies, a different ambience; or Roland Kirk, saxophones slung round his neck like the Ancient Mariner's albatross, sometimes playing three instruments at once, two of them—the strich and manzello—more or less his own inventions, while

simultaneously exhaling through a nose-flute. All are in their forties, except Kirk, born in 1936, the year Hitler threw tantrums at the Berlin Olympic Games because a black athlete, Jesse Owens, made a clean sweep of all the sprint events.

Insofar as these four musicians work regularly and profitably they are not typical of the average jazz player, whose living tends to be small as well as precarious. But they are equally vulnerable to the tilting of fashion. And the fact that two are black, two white, reflects a racial parity now commonplace in jazz. Yet despite the separate contributions of black and white musicians, jazz, just like the blues, until quite recently drew its vitality, its pattern of renewal, from inside the black communities of the United States. Militant black musicians, most of them avant-gardists, still see it that way, looking on their music— Black Music, they insist, not jazz—as part of the community's struggle for freedom. Yet the average Harlemite who queues outside the Apollo to catch James Brown has never heard of, let alone heard, Pharoah Sanders or even Archie Shepp. Black American society still revolves around the African practice of using music for dancing or ritual, never as an end in itself. Art is a Western concept, and the paradox is that the audience for Black Music, just as for straight jazz, is increasingly white, middle-class, often European as well. That audience is the key to the present and future of jazz. Some followers got sloughed off when beboppers complicated the music; the 1950s and 1960s found others opting for the hard-hitting beat of rock or soul rather than grappling with the subtleties of John Coltrane or the Modern Jazz Quartet. At the moment when jazz matured as an art form, spreading round the world, as international as ballet or cinema or sculpture, its audience started drying up in the place where everything began.

When Bob Brookmeyer was asked where jazz is heading, he replied: 'It's like your best girl asking "Will you still love me ten years from now?"' There is no safe or certain answer. One likelihood is that eclecticism will play as central a role as it is doing in

almost every art of our time. The television screen which unifies Marshal McLuhan's global village has an equally potent counterpart in the record shop, offering music from every century as well as every continent—Portuguese *fados*, Balinese gong music, Gregorian chant, Peking opera. Calling music 'serious' or 'popular' no longer corresponds to reality. The young British jazz composer, Michael Gibbs, admits that he listens to Charles Ives, Messaien and Crosby, Stills and Nash just as much as he does to jazz. Yet jazz remains unlike any other sort of music in its capacity to project the identity of a man, the uniqueness of his sound and style. That is why even the most brilliant musical collage—the Beatles' *Sergeant Pepper's Lonely Hearts Club Band*, for example—can have no parallel in jazz, simply because a jazz record exists to preserve a performance. Tapes may be spliced, musicians play duets with themselves, all sorts of artfulness go on, yet the truth can never be completely evaded. Jazz is about the people who play it. The fact seems especially important in the 1970s, a decade which looks like producing a music that is not exactly rock, not exactly jazz, but a mixture of the two. The greatest contribution jazz can make to such a fusion is not its musical sophistication, extensive though that is, but its intimacy, its personal scale. For jazz not only happens to be the toughest music around, it is also the most human.

*Eddie Gomez, bass virtuoso who came to prominence with the Bill Evans Trio. Overleaf Two off-beat reedmen. Left Yusef Lateef, who plays a variety of Oriental instruments as well as flute, tenor saxophone and oboe. Right Roland Kirk simultaneously blowing manzello (left), strich (centre) and tenor saxophone (right).*

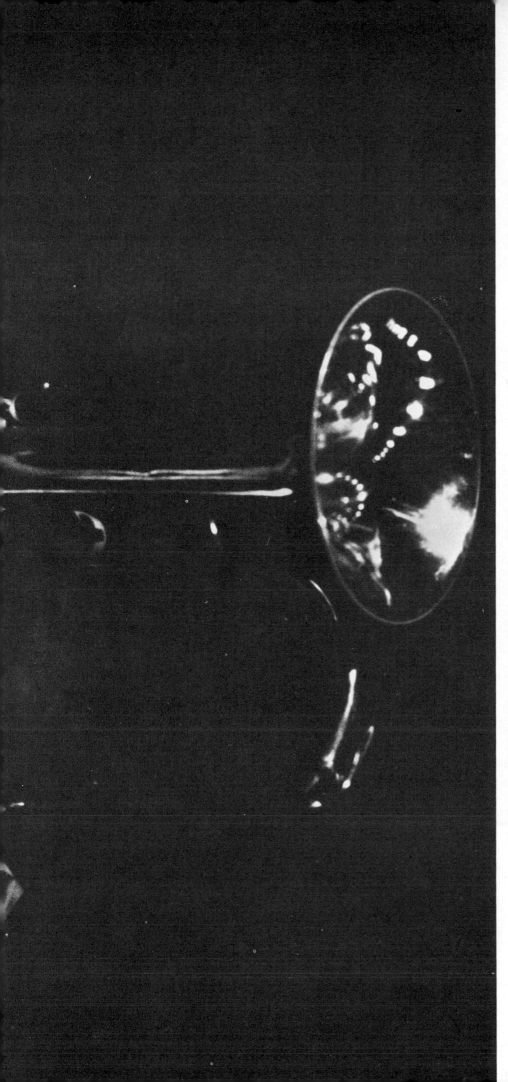

Left *Art Farmer, a leading trumpeter since the 1950s who now prefers to play the deeper-toned flugelhorn.* Top *Bobby Hutcherson, a vibraphonist with a style of his own.* Above *Bill Evans, the thinking man's pianist, unmatched at transforming a theme from within.* Overleaf *Archie Shepp relaxing.*

# Acknowledgments

*Colour*
Jean-Pierre Leloir 6, 102, 103; Record
Supervision Ltd – Tony Altaffer 99 (top left);
David Redfern Photography 2–3, 14 (centre),
14 (bottom), 22 (top left), 22 (top right), 22
(bottom), 23, 26–27, 27, 30, 31, 66–67, 70,
71, 74 (bottom), 75, 78 (left), 78 (right), 79,
107, 110, 111 (top), back jacket; Rex
Features Ltd 15; Frederick C. Warren 98;
Valerie Wilmer front jacket, 18–19, 74 (top),
106.

*Black and White*
Columbia Records 52 (top right), 52 (bottom
right); John Goldblatt 97; Peter Friedrich
Gorsen 7; Patrick Gwynn-Jones 9 (bottom);
Hans Harzheim 9 (top), 32 (top right), 56,
88–89, 96; Jazz Magazine – Giuseppe G. Pino
93 (top); Jan Perrson 8–9, 14 (top), 20–21,
29, 36 (centre), 43, 59, 61 (left), 72; David
Redfern Photography front endpaper, 1, 11, 76
(top right), 119 (bottom); The Robert
Stigwood Organisation Ltd 109; Valerie
Wilmer 10–11, 12, 13, 16 (left), 16 (right),
17, 20, 24 (left), 24 (right), 25, 28, 32 (top
left), 32 (bottom), 33, 34, 36 (top left), 36
(top right), 36 (bottom), 37, 38, 39, 40–41,
42 (left), 42 (right), 44, 46 (top), 46
(bottom), 46–47, 48–49, 49 (top), 49
(bottom), 50, 51, 52 (left), 54–55, 55 (left),
55 (right), 57, 58, 60, 61 (right), 62–63, 64,
65, 67 (top), 67 (bottom), 68 (top left),
68 (top right), 68 (bottom), 69, 71 (top),
71 (bottom), 73, 76 (left), 76 (bottom right),
77, 80, 81, 82 (top), 82 (bottom), 83, 84
(top), 84 (bottom), 85 (top), 85 (bottom),
86, 87, 88, 90, 91, 92 (top), 92 (bottom),
93 (bottom), 94 (left), 94 (right), 95, 99
(bottom left), 99 (right), 100–101, 104, 105
(top left), 105 (top right), 105 (bottom), 108,
111 (bottom), 112, 113, 115, 116, 117,
118–119, 119 (top), 120–121, back
endpapers.

# Bibliography

BALLIETT, Whitney, *The Sound of Surprise*.
Dutton, New York, 1959. Kimber, London,
1960. Penguin Books, 1963.
*Dinosaurs in the Morning*. Lippincott,
Philadelphia, 1962. Phoenix House, London,
1964.
*Such Sweet Thunder*. Bobbs-Merrill, New
York, 1966. Macdonald, London, 1968.
(Balliett is the most readable of jazz critics.
Nearly all the pieces in these volumes
appeared originally in the New Yorker.)
CHILTON, John, *Who's Who of Jazz:*
Storyville to Swing Street. The Bloomsbury
Book Shop, London, 1970. (Definitive
reference book of jazz musicians born before
1920.)
FEATHER, Leonard, *The Encyclopedia of Jazz*
(enlarged edition). Horizon Press, New York,
1960. Arthur Barker, London, 1961.
*The Encyclopedia of Jazz in the Sixties*.
Horizon Press, New York, 1966.
FOX, Charles, *Jazz in Perspective*. BBC
Publications, London, 1969. (A concise
chronological account of the development of
jazz.)
GILLETT, Charlie, *The Sound of the City:*
The Rise of Rock and Roll. Outerbridge &
Dientsfrey, New York, 1970. Souvenir Press,
London, 1971. (A scholarly survey of
happenings in pop music since the
mid-1950s, painstakingly researched and
especially good on black performers.)
GITLER, Ira, *Jazz Masters of the 40s*.
Macmillan, New York, 1966. (Detailed
assessments of Charlie Parker, Dizzy Gillespie
and other innovators. The same series
includes outstanding volumes on New
Orleans, by Martin Williams, and the Twenties,
by Richard Hadlock.)
HENTOFF, Nat, *The Jazz Life*. Dial Press,
New York, 1961. Peter Davies, London, 1962.
(Describes the working world of the jazz
musician.)
HODEIR, André, *Jazz: Its evolution and
essence*. Portulan, Paris (as *Hommes et
problèmes du jazz*) 1954. Grove Press, New
York, 1956. Secker & Warburg, London, 1956.
(Valuable analyses of jazz from 1930 to 1950s
but erratic on earlier periods.)
JONES, Leroi, *Blues People:* Negro music in
white America. Morrow, New York, 1963.
MacGibbon & Kee, London, 1965. (An
outline of jazz development by the
well-known black author and poet.)
*Black Music*. Morrow, New York, 1967.
MacGibbon and Kee, London, 1969. (Useful
essays on some of the new innovators – Cecil
Taylor, John Coltrane – but the later pieces
are subjective and partisan.)
JONES, Max, and CHILTON, John, *Louis*.
Studio Vista, London, 1971. (The story of
Louis Armstrong. Well documented and
illustrated.)
McCARTHY, Albert, MORGAN, Albun,
OLIVER, Paul and HARRISON, Max, *Jazz on
Record:* A critical guide to the first 50 years.

Hanover Books, London, 1968. Paperback
1971. (A reliable guide to the best jazz
records.)
McRAE, Barry, *The Jazz Cataclysm*. Dent,
London, 1967. Barnes, New York, 1967.
(Erratic but useful account of happenings
after the 1950s.)
NEWTON, Francis, *The Jazz Scene*.
MacGibbon & Kee, London, 1959. Monthly
Review Press, New York, 1960. Penguin
Books, 1961. (Good all-round coverage of
economic background as well as of
musicians.)
OLIVER, Paul, *Conversation with the Blues*.
Cassell, London, 1965. Horizon Press, New
York, 1965. (Interviews with American blues
performers.)
*The Story of the Blues*. Barrie & Rockliff,
London, 1969. (Splendidly documented and
illustrated survey of the blues.)
*Savannah Syncopators:* African Retentions in
the Blues. Studio Vista (paperback) London,
1970. (Valuable – and first-hand – theorising
on the African origin of jazz and blues.)
SCHULLER, Gunther, *Early Jazz*. Oxford
University Press, New York and London,
1968. (Covers jazz history up to 1931; the
best musicological study so far.)
SHAPIRO, Nat and HENTOFF, Nat, (eds)
*Hear Me Talkin' to Ya*. Rinehart, New York,
1955. Peter Davies, London, 1955. Penguin
Books, 1962. (The history of jazz in the words
of the musicians themselves.)
SPELLMAN, A. B. *Four Lives in the Bebop
Business*. Pantheon Books, New York, 1966.
MacGibbon & Kee, London, 1967. (Studies,
by a black jazz writer, of Ornette Coleman,
Jackie McLean, Herbie Nichols and Cecil
Taylor.)
STEARNS, Marshall, *The Story of Jazz*.
Oxford University Press, New York, 1956.
Sidgwick & Jackson, London, 1957.
Paperback 1958. (Excellent general history.)
WILLIAMS, Martin, *The Jazz Tradition*.
Oxford University Press, New York and
London, 1970. (Essays on sixteen important
musicians from Jelly Roll Morton to Ornette
Coleman.)
WILMER, Valerie, *Jazz People*. Allison &
Busby, London, 1970. (Interviews with
fourteen musicians, including Big Joe Turner
and Buck Clayton as well as Cecil Taylor,
Don Cherry and Thelonious Monk.)

# Index